NYPD
BATTLES
CRIME

Advisor in Criminal Justice to Northeastern University Press
GILBERT GEIS

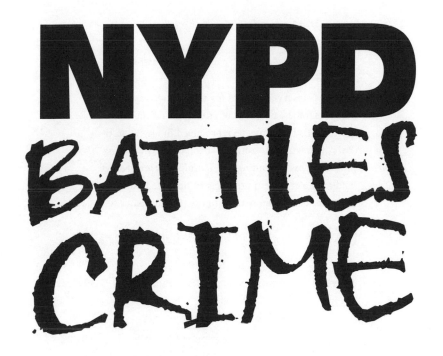

NYPD BATTLES CRIME

INNOVATIVE STRATEGIES IN POLICING

ELI B. SILVERMAN

NORTHEASTERN UNIVERSITY PRESS • Boston

Northeastern University Press

Library of Congress Cataloging-in-Publication Data

Silverman, Eli B., 1939–
NYPD battles crime : innovative strategies in policing / Eli B. Silverman.
p. cm.
Includes bibliographical references.
ISBN 1-55553-401-5 (pbk. : alk. paper)
ISBN 1-55553-402-3 (cl. : alk. paper)
1. New York (N.Y.). Police Dept.   2. Police—New York (State)—
New York.   3. Police-community relations—New York (State)—New
York.   4. Crime—New York (State)—New York.   5. Crime
prevention—New York (State)—New York.   6. Criminal investigation—New
York (State)—New York—Data processing.
I. Title.
HV8148.N5S56   1999
363.2′09747—DC21   99-17514

Designed by Janice Wheeler

Composed in Trump Medieval by G&S Typesetters, Inc., Austin, Texas.
Printed and bound by Maple Press, York, Pennsylvania.
The paper is Sebago Antique, an acid-free sheet.

MANUFACTURED IN THE UNITED STATES OF AMERICA
03 02 01 00 99   5 4 3 2 1

My wife, Susan Tackel, has willingly served many roles—inspiration, critic, suggester, supporter, and endurer of my nighttime writing and police ride-alongs. She has lovingly sacrificed time and sleep. I am forever grateful.

.

In loving memory of my parents, David and Dianne Silverman, and my beloved brother Jerry

CONTENTS

ACKNOWLEDGMENTS

Navigating the waters separating the academic and police worlds can be treacherous. Both sides were puzzled by my frequent early-morning visits to police crime-fighting strategy meetings. Colleagues noted that "if you've seen one meeting, you've seen them all." Police inquired why someone in his right mind, no less a college professor, would willingly arise in time to attend 7 A.M. meetings! Thanks to recent NYPD advances in sharing information, academic and police currents are far more confluent today.

President Gerald W. Lynch of John Jay College of Criminal Justice graciously provided vigorous encouragement and sabbatical support. Provost Basil Wilson energetically supported my research through funding and computer assistance. Graduate Dean James Levine enthusiastically peppered me with references and reassurances. Professor Andrew Karmen effectively shepherded John Jay's multidisciplined study of New York City's crime decline. Members of my own Department of Law and Police Science have been constant sources of insightful analysis. The department's chairs, Professors T. Kenneth Moran and Robert McCrie, provided encouragement and support.

This book could not have been written without the unusual cooperation and access granted to me by the New York City Police Department. Commissioner Howard Safir, who embodies the department motto of "courtesy, professionalism, and respect," has graciously welcomed my research. His predecessor, William J. Bratton, welcomed and encouraged academic inquiry into the NYPD.

I am greatly indebted to the hundreds of police officials, both at headquarters and in the field, particularly the Brooklyn North Patrol Borough, who have endured my numerous questions, endless attendance at meetings, and field observations. Although I cannot mention everyone by name, each provided unique assistance, encouragement, and support. I am especially grateful to Chief of Department Louis R. Anemone, First Deputy Commissioner Patrick E. Kelleher, former Police Commissioner Patrick V. Murphy, former First Deputy Commissioner John F. Timoney, Deputy Commissioner for Operations Edward T. Norris, former Deputy Commissioner for Operations Jack Maple, Chief of Organized Crime Control Martin O'Boyle, Chief of Detectives William H. Allee, Jr., Deputy Commissioner for Policy and Planning Michael J. Farrell, Deputy Commissioner for Legal Matters George A. Grasso, Housing Bureau Chief Joseph P. Dunne, Deputy Chief Alfred J. Materasso, Deputy Chief John Laffey, Deputy Chief Joseph P. Raguso, Deputy Chief Michael Tiffany, Assistant Commissioner Philip G. McGuire, Inspector Edwin A. Young, Inspector Edward Cannon, Inspector Michael Collins, Inspector Anthony Marra, Deputy Inspector Michael J. Mandel, Deputy Inspector Gordon Nash, Deputy Inspector Joseph Cuneen, Deputy Inspector Raymond A. Redmond, Deputy Inspector Garry F. McCarthy, Managing Attorney Robert F. Messner, Director of Training Dr. James O'Keefe, Captain Ronald Shindel, Captain William F. Chimento, Captain Bill Gorta, Lieutenant Frank Dwyer, Lieutenant Ray Manus, Lieutenant Edward Forsyth, Lieutenant Robert Knoth, Sergeant Gene Whyte, Sergeant John Yohe, Detective Joe Falletta, Sergeant Paul Scott, Sergeant Vennasa Ferro, Sergeant Yalkin Demirkaya, Detective Jill Tomczak, and computer associate Kathy Costello.

The fact that so many of these police officials and others who appear in the book have since risen to more advanced positions is a testimony to their commitment and integrity. These qualities radiate throughout the department down to the street patrol level.

I have been fortunate to have had the advice and guidance of William A. Frohlich, director of Northeastern University Press, the expertise of the press's staff, including Ann Twombly, Tara Mantel, and Jill Bahcall, and the skills of their copy editor Deborah Kops.

Professor Gil Geis was an exceptional reader, reviewer, and critic. I am indebted to his inspiration, commitment, and encouragement. Paul O'Connell provided guidance, insight, and collaboration on NYPD operations. Rob Lawson supplied imagination, perseverance, optimism, and friendship. Peter Ohlhausen masterfully critiqued concepts and details. Mary Hapel provided unending research, typing, and enthusiasm. Gilda Meklosky adroitly unearthed buried information. Professor James Fyfe insightfully reviewed the book proposal. Professor Joseph Viteritti provided valuable insight and reflection. Peter Dodenhoff, Deidre Williams, Sydney Joshua, Steve Kline, Steve Nash, Karen Bloomquist, and Susan Fuller furnished valuable assistance. Michael Gordon contributed the fine cover photograph. Karin Otto supplied artistic inspiration. Marty Jezer provided fine and thorough indexing. To all, I acknowlege a great debt. Any errors that may have found their way into the text are mine.

I am especially grateful to my family—my wife, Susan Tackel, son Mark, daughter Karin, sister- and brother-in-law Judith and David Tabb, their son Jonah, brother-in-law Philip Tackel, mother-in-law Mildred Tackel—and many friends here and abroad for their indulgence and support throughout this project.

A special thank-you to Bob and Laura Tucker, their son Ben, Richard Blazej, Lucy Spahr-Blazej, and their sons Andrew and Matt for their Vermont hospitality, writing haven, and clarinet playing.

NYPD BATTLES CRIME

1   JUMPING THE TURNSTILE

11 P.M., March 26, 1996.
Scene: A dark corridor at the 116th Street subway station on the Lexington Avenue line, in New York City.

The rumble of an approaching train sounds from the lower level. A lanky, twenty-two-year-old man, five feet ten inches tall, 140 pounds, neatly dressed, and carrying a backpack, vaults the turnstile and descends into the subway. Anthony Downing, an undercover transit cop with the New York City Police Department (NYPD), arrests the man and takes him to the East 119th Street station house, where he is fingerprinted and released.

Officer Downing recalled being struck by how completely calm the man was and remembered that he had no police record. Beth Lyons, a Legal Aid lawyer who subsequently represented the man on the turnstile-jumping charge, did not remember him at a later date because "It was such a minor offense." [1]

John Royster was arrested on June 12, 1996—one day after the brutal slaying of Evelyn Alvarez, a beloved Park Avenue dry cleaner. Alvarez, known as the Lollipop Lady because she gave treats to kids, was not Royster's only victim. He was also charged with savagely assaulting four other women during an eight-day crime spree. Two of the more vicious of these acts were the attack and disfigurement of a fifty-one-year-old publicist, who was jogging on Manhattan's exclusive Upper East Side, and the assault and attempted rape in Central Park of a thirty-two-year-old pianist. Royster was found guilty of murder and aggravated assault in March 1998.

The incriminating evidence was Royster's fingerprint. Was it a lucky break? Not really. The NYPD found the print because refined communications enabled the department to connect the dots. Royster's fingerprint card from the turnstile incident was scanned into the computer, and it matched bloodied prints lifted from a window at the scene of the Park Avenue killing.

Royster joins a growing number of criminals who have been caught by a newly constituted NYPD, characterized by intensely focused investigations, heightened internal communications, and decentralized management. Royster's arrest represents New York City's full-court press on crime, whose sharp decline has made international headlines and enhanced the reputations of two police commissioners and a mayor.

Reversing the Trend

"We Pace U.S. Crime Cut," heralded the *Daily News,* New York City's tabloid paper. A more than 9 percent decrease in crime for 1997 falls just 1 percent short of extending the city's unprecedented double-digit crime decline for each of the preceding three years. Mayor Rudolph Giuliani proudly proclaimed, "Much of America's crime drop is attributed to New York City."[2]

The city's five-year, 50.5 percent plummet in major crimes places the NYPD at the epicenter of competing claims. The department and its supporters assume prime responsibility for the dramatic crime drop. The normally reserved *New York Times* describes the NYPD as "simply breathtaking" and "a marvel of

American law enforcement."[3] A comment by the *Sun Herald* of Sydney, Australia, typifies the international acclaim heaped on the department: "New York has achieved an astounding turn-around in the incidence of every type of crime."[4]

Police forces throughout the world observe and then imitate the so-called New York Police Model. "Virtually every other city," notes *Newsweek*, "looks to borrow from New York's crime strategy."[5] In Connecticut, Hartford's police chief declares: "We're doing it just like they're doing it in New York. I hate to sound like a copycat, but why waste time reinventing the wheel?"[6] After the mayor of Washington, D.C., visits the NYPD, newspaper headlines announce, "Mayor Gets His New York–Style Anti-Crime Initiative Underway."[7]

When New York recorded its 1994 crime statistics, the decline's reality and permanence, and the NYPD's contribution, were all viewed with scholarly skepticism. Many commentators stressed prevailing social, economic, and demographic conditions as core contributors to the drop. One researcher, for example, asserted that crime rates in large cities can be predicted accurately 80 to 90 percent of the time by looking at economic and social factors such as income, unemployment, education, the prevalence of minorities and of households headed by single women, household size, and home ownership.[8] But sustained crime drops, new police initiatives, and the inadequacy of socioeconomic explanations have transformed staunch resistance into reluctant acknowledgment of the impact of the police.

An effective NYPD presence on the streets is reducing crime. John Jay College Professor Andrew Karmen clearly demonstrates that New York City homicides committed out-of-doors with guns fell more abruptly than those committed indoors or with knives or other weapons. Karmen's analysis also shows that increased patrol strength and rises in misdemeanor arrests for quality-of-life offenses are associated with homicide declines.[9] Quality-of-life crimes include such traditional petty offenses as loitering, peddling, creating loud noises, defacing with graffiti, and other incivilities that violate people's sense of well-being.

And yet, regardless of how much credit the NYPD gets, the Madison Avenue–style claims and publicity surrounding it far exceed the amount of serious analysis focused on NYPD's concrete departmental changes. What has the NYPD done so differently since 1994 to reduce crime this dramatically? Will it be able to continue to produce a downturn in crime? These questions are at the core of this book, which is an account of organizational change and continuity, innovation and preservation. Many of the post-1993 NYPD reforms are a culmination of earlier reform efforts, dramatically reconfigured and energized from within the department. They are set in the context of varying crime rates and the advent of so-called new policing.

The New Reality

New York City's 12 percent crime decline in 1994 (compared to a national drop of less than 2 percent) grew to 16 percent in 1995 and remained 16 percent in 1996. These decreases accounted for more than 60 percent of the national decline. Over a five-year period, overall rates for murder, rape, robbery, felonious assault, burglary, grand larceny, and motor vehicle theft plunged 50.5 percent. New York can justifiably claim to be the major force driving down the nation's crime rate. The figures are striking, as Table 1 indicates.

To appreciate the magnitude of this decline, one need only consider the 67 percent drop in New York's homicide rate (believed to be the most accurate of crime statistics). The number of murders declined from over 2,200 in 1990 to about 1,500 in 1994, 1,200 in 1995, 984 in 1996, 767 in 1997, and 629 in 1998. Chicago (with less than one-third of New York City's population) had more homicides (695) in 1998 than did New York.

Table 1
Decrease in Crimes in New York City from 1993 to 1998

Against the Person (%)		Against Property (%)	
Murder	−67	Burglary	−53
Rape	−23	Grand larceny	−40
Robbery	−54	Motor vehicle theft	−61
Felonious Assault	−29		

Because of this phenomenal drop in its crime rate, New York City's crime ranking has declined. In a five-year period (1994 to 1998), New York dropped from a position of 114th to 163rd in the ranking of the 200 most dangerous U.S. cities with populations above 100,000. In short, New York is now safer than Dallas, Houston, Los Angeles, Baltimore, Washington, and Philadelphia. And New York has proportionally less crime than such smaller cities as Phoenix, Memphis, Seattle, Fort Lauderdale, Denver, San Diego, Albany, San Francisco, and Boise. "Crime-drop doubters" now concede a change has occurred. As Franklin Zimring, a renowned criminologist at the University of California at Berkeley, acknowledged, "I have been a skeptic but now, because of the length of the decline and its magnitude, . . . I think I am experiencing a foxhole conversion."[10]

Some, however, have questioned the accuracy of crime data—which, of course, is crucial. With New York City crime rates plummeting and pressure being put on commanders to maintain those low levels, allegations have been raised regarding the precision of police crime recording and classification. There is no denying this pressure. The question is, have officials distorted the figures more in the last several years than before? There seems to be no evidence of this.

The department has beefed up its auditing of crime reporting. The Investigation and Evaluation Unit, which traditionally has monitored misconduct cases, is now, with additional personnel, also monitoring precinct reporting of crime categories such as lost property and petit larceny. They are especially sensitive to downgrading of crimes. These reports are prepared not only for the chief of patrol but for—and under the direction of—the chief of the department. Precinct commanding officers must account for classification practices.

The department has also added a Data Integrity Unit in Deputy Commissioner Michael Farrell's Office of Management Analysis and Planning. This unit systematically reviews precinct crime recording. These reviews are regularly discussed at crime-fighting strategy meetings. In addition, headquarters insists that commanders review each crime complaint report in their command. So the pressure is not only to produce but to produce honestly.

Furthermore, each borough and precinct is held responsible for the integrity of its own crime reporting. In October 1996 a Bronx borough audit revealed that one of its precinct commanders falsified reports by listing some crimes as misdemeanors instead of felonies in order to improve his statistics. The commander is no longer with the department. In this and other scattered cases, the department has uncovered inaccuracies. Although some crimes may be deliberately or inadvertently misclassified, other crimes such as homicide are very difficult to deliberately misclassify or ignore.

Fluctuating Forces

Understanding crime rates is difficult, especially when there is a sudden, sharp decline, as in the current New York City experience. Orthodox criminological explanations tend not to be up to the task, and flawed analysis only spawns more conjecture. As a result, the criminological explanation undergoes periodic reshuffling, and the reader is free to choose any combination of options.

Conventional Explanations

A FLUCTUATING YOUTH POPULATION Criminologists traditionally look to fluctuations in the youth population as a key to interpreting crime rates. Since youngsters commit a disproportionate share of the nation's crime, statisticians assume that more young people means more crime. In 1990, the well-known criminologist James Q. Wilson observed, "Troublesome people quiet down as they get older. Many of us predict that in the early 1990s, with more children of the baby boom being born, the crime rate will continue to rise no matter what the government does."[11] Several years later, Princeton criminologist John DiIulio all but guaranteed a new generation of hard-core criminals by the year 2000. According to DiIulio, this group would consist primarily of an additional 500,000 males between the ages of fourteen and seventeen who, raised in poverty, are "the youngest, biggest, and baddest generation that any society has ever known."[12] The notion of a future explosion in the crime-prone population has also crept into the lexicon of media commentators. Writing in 1995, the respected columnist Neal R. Peirce observed that police will "have to run just to stay even. We're soon to experience a baby boom 'echo' with 23 percent more teens aged 14 to 17—precisely the group in which murder rates have been accelerating because of family breakdown, drugs, television violence and the growing number and firepower of guns."[13]

Yet there are no data to support the thesis that a sharp decline in New York City's fifteen- to nineteen-year-old population is the reason for New York's recent crime drop. For the 1993–1996 period, the number of youths in this age bracket increased slightly, advancing one study's conclusion that "the size of the city's youth population does not appear to be a universally reliable indicator of the changes in the crime rate." [14] The New York City Department of City Planning, moreover, forecasts a relatively constant population level for this age group through the year 2000.

A RISE IN INCARCERATION RATES   Incarceration rates are also a fertile source for explanations of the crime rate decline. While the New York State prison population has risen during the three-year period in question, it has done so at the modest annual rate of 7.8 percent—hardly enough to reduce crime significantly. Furthermore, the number of annual new additions to the prison system actually declined 10.3 percent during this period, with city residents constituting a stable 70 percent of the annual state prison admissions in recent years. The number of inmates serving sentences of one year or less for misdemeanor convictions in the city's jails has remained stable for these three years. The number of those paroled from state prison in the same period has also been relatively stable, despite an increase of 7.2 percent in the probation population. Since some probationers commit additional crimes, this modest rise offers no support for the assertion that a swelling of the numbers in the corrections system explains the city's crime drop. In addition, New York's prison growth rate ranks as the nation's third lowest from 1992 to 1997. It makes little sense, moreover, to consider incarceration rates separately from police activity resulting in arrests. [15]

INCREASING UNEMPLOYMENT   Crime is customarily considered an alternative path for the unemployed. But New York City's employment picture is quite mixed. While the number of people employed rose steadily between 1995 and 1997, for example, the unemployment rate shot up. In other words, the labor force increased during this period even as more people were looking for work and not finding it.

To illustrate, the number employed in New York City, according to the U.S. Bureau of Labor Statistics, grew from 2,925,279 in 1995 to 2,982,010 in 1996 and 3,056,225 in 1997. At the same time, however, the city's unemployment rate increased from 8.2 percent in 1995 to 8.8 percent in 1996 and 9.4 percent in 1997. The city's advancing rate occurred while the nation's unemployment rate declined from 5.6 percent in 1995 to 5.4 percent in 1996 and 4.9 percent in 1997. The city's declining crime rate in the midst of steadily increasing unemployment rates raises serious doubts about the criminal employment opportunity thesis. This incongruity is even more pronounced when one considers that although the less skilled and less educated bear the brunt of unemployment, the neighborhoods in which they live (low-income, low-educational-level precincts) have seen a disproportionately greater decrease in crime.

IMPROVED MEDICAL CARE   Another explanation for the crime-rate drop is medical. The argument states that wounded victims who in the past would have died now often survive as a result of extraordinary improvements in medical care at crime scenes and in ambulances, trauma centers, emergency rooms, and intensive care units. Even with the same level of violence occurring, such persons, because they survive, would be recorded as victims of aggravated assault, not homicide, thus reducing the overall homicide rate. The problem with that argument, however, is that in a study of emergency medical services (EMS) in eight cities, the National Institute of Justice (NIJ) did not find increases in aggravated assaults. Moreover, victims of attempting murderers typically do not survive. A coroner in one city noted that he couldn't remember the last time he "encountered a shooting victim who had been shot only once."[16]

Similarly, an examination of New York City's EMS failed to find a strong impact on the homicide rate. During the 1993–1994 period, for example, Karmen found that "the small number of presumably saved lives augmenting the ranks of assault victims is trivial when compared to the much larger number of persons routinely wounded by assailants each year." Nor was there a sudden rise in the proportion of victims already dead before medical help arrived or a shift in the percentage of victims dead on arrival after the ambulance ride or of those who expired in the emergency room, the intensive care unit, or elsewhere in the hospital.[17]

REDUCED DRUG ACTIVITY   A drop in drug activity is often offered as another explanation for the decrease in crime. However, the NIJ study of homicides in eight U.S. cities (not including New York) between 1985 and 1994 did not find an association between the homicide rate and the level of use of such drugs as PCP, LSD, heroin, and marijuana.[18]

Crack addiction, however, *is* more generally associated with criminal behavior. The Drug Use Forecasting (DUF) program, which examines arrestee drug use, records escalating crack levels throughout the nation during the late 1980s, then a steady decline. The initial, late-1980s explosion in the number of crack addicts, some contend, inflated the crime rate, which subsequently declined during the 1990s. The evidence is mixed for New York. Manhattan DUF data show a "substantial decline" in youth cocaine/crack arrestees from 1989 to 1994 (young people are more likely to smoke marijuana). At the same time, there was a "relatively constant (and typically high) rate" of cocaine and crack use among adult arrestees.[19]

While the number of youthful drug offenders has declined, arrests of offenders in New York for drug use remained stable from 1993 to 1995 and then increased in 1996 to a level surpassing the zenith of the crack epidemic of 1988–1989. Despite these fluctuations, New York homicides plunged, thereby downplaying another explanation.

Trendy Takes.   "Maturing" drug markets, say some ethnographers, are the key to the mystery of declining crime. In the 1980s, according to this theory, inner-city drug markets involved numerous inept suppliers and distributors who either were new to the market or had previously traded heroin or marijuana, not crack. After a wave of street violence and a decline in clients, the drug trade became more structured and organized in the 1990s. There were fewer retailers, supply systems were consolidated, and much of the street drug trade moved indoors to bodegas, video stores, and groceries. Indoor drug dealing generated fewer turf battles, drive-by shootings, and neighborhood violence.[20] These observations, however, scarcely acknowledge the role of police operations in shutting down outdoor drug operations.

The "Little Brother Syndrome," like the drug market thesis, is an explanation that does not rely on police performance. Today's youth, it contends, are turned off to drugs and crime because they have witnessed the violence and death that have befallen their older siblings.[21] That may very well be true, but little brothers may also wish to avoid incarceration or police arrests. In either case, one must await further research.

Moving On.   There is at best limited support for the various hypotheses offered for the nation's most dramatic crime decline. These explanations have been found wanting or, at the minimum, in need of fuller documentation. Those who ignore the importance of the role of the police in the decline of crime seem to subscribe to a kind of criminal justice "big bang" theory— that an impromptu, unpredictable, undocumented constellation of forces suddenly emerged to drive New York City's crime down at an unprecedented rate. Yet, in one of the few comprehensive reviews of crime reduction in New York (primarily gun crimes), the 1996 Citizens Crime Commission report concluded, "In sum, decreased crime reporting, demographic changes, developments in the drug trade, national trends or the local economy do not appear to offer adequate explanations for the recent decreases in crime in New York City."[22] The plummeting of New York's crime rates since 1993 provides a dramatic demonstration that more is at work than can be explained by comparatively glacial changes in the social fabric.

Academic explanations have given way to intellectual humility. An editor of a scholarly journal recently wrote, "Over the last two decades, criminologists have had an attack of conscience. Humbled by past theoretical mistakes, some major and others simply naive, we are properly wary of imposing our limited insights on the world."[23] The criminologist John DiIulio echoed this observation: "This is a humbling time for all crime analysts."[24] The criminological view that "without profound changes in society, there isn't much anyone can do about crime" is under attack. "Suddenly, new facts have turned this accepted wisdom on its head."[25]

The New Policing

As the naysayers have been reduced to debating not whether but how much credit should be given to the police, a fresh recognition of a new and successful policing strategy is emerging. Reflecting on this phenomenon, the columnist Neal Peirce notes criminologists' failure to predict the nationwide decline in crime and their inadequate "after the fact explanations. . . . Crime is dropping much too fast, too rapidly in multiple major cities for such explanations to suffice. . . . Smarter, reinvented policing" provides the key.[26]

But what is the nature of this NYPD model and its "smarter, reinvented policing"? Has one overconfident dogma been substituted for another? *Business Week* extols the NYPD's "businesslike crime-fighting" approach.[27] *Forbes* credits the NYPD's "brilliant reorganization" and "remolding."[28] A *Time* cover story focuses on quality-of-life crimes and arrests.[29] After months in New York, a British police superintendent reports on a change in the "culture of the NYPD from one which tacitly accepted an ever growing major crime rate to one where . . . crime can be fought and beaten back."[30]

Media accolades have been exceeded only by NYPD swagger. The department claims it has profited from a "sea change in the way it does business."[31] The former NYPD commissioner William Bratton rhetorically asks, "Why are the steep declines in crime happening at this time?" His expansive response credits "fundamental changes in management philosophy and operating principles. We have gone from a micro-managed organization with very little strategic direction to a decentralized management style with strong strategic guidance at the top."[32] Looking back on his work, Commissioner Bratton stresses the importance of ambitious, concrete goals and the vital role of modern managerial reengineering teams. "We reengineered the NYPD into an organization capable of supporting our goals,"[33] he observes. But turnarounds do not happen overnight. Large-city police departments typically feature such organizational barriers as a complex hierarchy, specialization, and a plethora of rules. NYPD's organizational change has been evolutionary, a series of events leading slowly to a major reformation.

An Evolutionary Event.   It took eighty years for police departments to reconfigure from the decentralized, politically dominated social service agencies that they were at the turn of the century and to become today's bureaucratic, professional, more centralized, and exclusively law enforcement organizations. This evolutionary period—from about 1890 through 1970—encompassed two separate, although overlapping, periods of major transformations, which rank among "the foremost examples of institutional change in urban America."[34] These changes affected police functions and responsibilities, personnel recruitment, and organizational structure.

It is helpful to note two critical aspects of these changes. The first is their extraordinarily lengthy time spans. The first period of change occurred from 1890 to 1930; the second between 1930 and the late 1960s. The other interesting aspect is that only the latter period saw internally planned organizational change.

The first era (1890 to 1930) yielded departmental centralization that was externally induced and hence unplanned by the police organizations. Urban police leaders, galvanized by corruption scandals and dissatisfied with the politically dominated, corrupt, unprofessional operations of their departments, were pushed toward reform by outside commercial, civic, and religious groups. During this first era of reform, large-city police departments such as New York's slowly and imperfectly adapted to the demands of these outside reformers.

The second reform period (1930 to the late 1960s), on the other hand, was introduced by law enforcement leaders who were inspired by new business- and scientific-management models. The leaders sought to confine the police to strict law enforcement and to curb their social service activities. This was to be accomplished through more specialized, centralized, clearly defined professional and organizational roles. Police leadership had the benefit of both previous and contemporary external support and a forty-year reform campaign.

Post 1970. Since the late 1960s and early 1970s, another reform, the community policing–problem solving model, has emerged. Two prominent proponents label community policing the "first major reform in policing since police departments embraced scientific management principles more than a half century ago."[35] Although the movement is not easily defined,[36] community policing's most frequently cited characteristics are joint community-police crime prevention, decreased authoritarianism, and increased organizational flexibility and decentralization.[37] Despite the extensive literature related to the advantages of community policing, there is little firm information about how widely it has been adopted. In 1992, one academic conceded, "How little systematic knowledge we have of changes in police organizations in this country . . . even short run changes."[38] It is no wonder that developments three years later led astute scholars to observe, "Much of what now passes for community policing is but a pale imitation of the grand vision . . . touching ground only through marginally significant new programs, such as bicycle patrols or mini–police stations." [39]

A recent systematic survey assessed the extent to which 228 police departments have embraced the community policing model. The survey examined an extensive array of independent organizational and external factors that affect policing functions and practices. [40] These factors were examined to see their impact on various police programs, such as foot, bicycle, or horse patrol; storefront police stations; task units for solving special problems in targeted areas; fixed assignment of officers to neighborhoods; and administrative changes, such as increased hiring of civilians and greater patrol officer responsibilities. Significantly, as of 1996, the study had found scant evidence of fundamental change in police organizations. However, the survey found plenty of support for the thesis that the professional-bureaucratic authoritarian model has persisted: "The core mission has remained largely unchanged during the past 50 years or more . . . little substantial organizational structural change has taken place in American policing in recent years, despite all of the discussion about community policing. This means that American policing is likely engaged in a long process of evolution rather than a fast-moving revolution. . . . It appears to be more creeping incrementalism than decisive advancement." [41]

Conclusion

It is not surprising that reform is difficult, in part because large police departments operate like other large organizations. The essential components of the professional-bureaucratic model have traditionally produced the organizational armor used to ward off attacks by reformers. Specialist units composed of detectives and narcotics officers, for instance, have been incessantly criticized for their separation from the bulk of the department's main contingent—its patrol force—thereby hindering their common crime-fighting efforts. Yet this relationship has remained, until recently, fairly static, with each unit charting its own distinct course. Before the 1990s, units were more frequently assessed by their own productivity than by their impact on crime in general. Patrol was measured by response times to calls for service or by arrests; traffic, by the number of violations or car stops; and detectives, by their case clearance record. The need for better integration was clear, but top-down, rule-oriented, rigidly layered, fragmented police bureaucracies have long provided a protective covering for inadequate specialist-generalist coordination and information sharing.

When critics maintain that administrative inflexibilities inhibit police from focusing on citizen concerns,[42] departments react predictably with adaptive devices that effect superficial fixes. These changes take the form of "boundary spanning"—isolated, special units such as community affairs offices that reach out to their surrounding communities without significantly altering core police missions or practices. In the past, the NYPD devised special image-driven, quickie training programs or projects such as high-visibility foot patrol or mini-stations to ward off external criticism.[43]

Scholars of policing have shown that the police's unique occupational role contributes to insularity, defensiveness, organizational routine, and cautiousness. Conflict and ambivalence pervade the police function. An officer is frequently subject to incompatible missions, such as law enforcement, order maintenance, peacekeeping, and fear reduction.[44] Citizens, moreover, are often ambivalent about the police—wanting them to be available when somebody else is breaking the law, but not wanting to be bothered when speeding, for example. As Egon Bittner observes, the public suspects that "there is something of the dragon in the dragon slayer."[45] Abnormal working hours and life-threatening situations promote an officer's association and identification with other officers. It is a dangerous world out there for the police, and that world is increasingly viewed in "us versus them" terms. Caution and ambivalence grow when officers see arrested perpetrators slip unpunished through the criminal justice system, when officers interact with an ambivalent public,[46] and when the department hierarchy adheres to rigid organizational rules if officers employ their wide discretion in unwise or unpopular ways.[47]

Their perception of inadequate public and top-level organizational support not only increases police officers' solidarity and isolation, but also decreases organizational inventiveness and risk taking. Fundamental change in policing, then, has had a tortured and difficult past. One review of attempts to alter the rank structure of police departments has compared the endeavor to "bending granite."[48] Progress is extremely difficult and, if history is any guide, requires internal and external support as well as generations of committed, reform-minded people.

These forces coalesced in 1994 as part of an unassuming departmental crime strategy meeting known as Compstat, which grew to wield enormous influence over the NYPD revolution. Driven by intelligence gathering and fueled by innovative managerial processes, this engine of change has jolted the NYPD bureaucracy and has propelled it to new crime-fighting heights. These post-1993 developments of the New York City Police Department can best be appreciated in the context of its earlier reform struggles. It is to this subject that we now turn.

2   THE PRE-1984 NYPD
Reform and Resistance

Patrick V. Murphy had served eighteen months as the NYPD's reform commissioner, curbing "widespread corruption"[1] and modernizing the department's style of management. Then on Friday, April 14, 1972, an episode launched a period that Murphy considered his administration's "low point":[2] At 11:41 A.M., a call was made to 911 by a "Detective Thomas of the 2-8 Precinct," reporting a 10-13 (officer in trouble) on the second floor at 102 West 116th Street. This call did more than light up the police switchboard; it unleashed an avalanche of events and passions that resounded for years throughout the city's law enforcement landscape.

The Harlem Mosque Murder

The address turned out to be that of a Black Muslim mosque. The first of many police to reach 102 West 116th Street were Officers Philip Cardillo and Vito Navarra of the 28th Precinct. Despite differing versions, observers agreed that a scuffle inside resulted in the shooting of the two officers. One of them, Cardillo, died six days later.

As more police responded, a crowd grew outside the mosque, fueled by rumors of what was happening inside. The *New York*

Times reported that the event was marked by "three hours of in-termittent disorder in the surrounding Harlem streets. The city's first substantial racial disturbance this year. . . . [T]he oaths and bottles flew through the spring air as a thousand people milled around the mosque. . . ."[3] Reporters were attacked, and an un-marked police car was overturned and set on fire.

The episode brought to light ideological differences within the NYPD. To the cop on the street and to Robert Daley, the depart-ment's deputy commissioner of public information (who was on the scene), Officer Cardillo was doing his job when he was shot by a Muslim at close range, possibly with the officer's own gun. Daley estimated that 1,200 people were milling in the streets within a one-block area.

At the hospital where Cardillo lay in intensive care, Daley recounted the events to Mayor John Lindsay and Commissioner Murphy, characterizing the incident as a racial riot. Both vehe-mently disagreed with his assessment. Said Lindsay, "Riot? What do you mean riot? There can't be any riot. How can you say such things?" Murphy downplayed the event, saying, "We had reports it wasn't so bad there."[4] The reform commissioner later recalled a bulging-eyed Daley drawing the attention of bystand-ers as he ran down the hall shouting in a high-pitched voice, "There's a riot out there. Don't you know that?" Lindsay, accord-ing to Murphy, bore down on the "out-of-control" deputy com-missioner: "How do you know it's a riot? How can it be a riot if it's under control?"[5]

Daley felt it was in the department's interest to release the full truth, and the sooner the better. Concealment, in his view, only lent support to the Muslims' version of events. Sure enough, on Sunday, two days after the incident, in a *New York Times* feature story ("Muslim Minister Assails Police Action"), the Muslim minister Louis Farrakhan charged that the police had committed an "unprovoked, wanton and possible premeditated attack" on a house of worship. Included in the story was this statement from

Commissioner Murphy: "A vicious, anonymous phone call was responsible for yesterday's terrible tragedy. . . . [T]he call resulted in pushing and shoving which turned into a fight which did not end until one policeman was shot and critically wounded and a number of other persons were injured."[6] Daley, eager to publicize the department's point of view, dismissed the statement, calling it "a brief communiqué, which clarified nothing."[7]

The following day, the commissioner publicly discussed the issue and defended the actions of the police. When asked if the police had acted properly, Murphy responded, "We can all quarterback on Monday morning and say, 'I might have done it a little differently,' but I have no question about the motives and dedication of the police officers."[8]

To the NYPD rank and file, Murphy's statement soared like a lead balloon. Why, they wondered, was there no reference to the provocative behavior and irresponsibility of the inhabitants of the mosque? Where in the official statement was support for the police doing their jobs? Furthermore, they believed the department was restraining proper crime scene investigation of this tragedy. In a book about the events, a former NYPD detective (who was at the mosque) and his co-author relentlessly detailed the injustices the police felt they had suffered at the hands of their leaders: Outside "political influence" impinged on appropriate crime-scene photos; police were impeded from adequately securing the crime scene and physical evidence; and suspects were permitted to leave the mosque and remain at large, on their honor to show up later, which they failed to do.[9] Surely, the street cops believed, stronger statements and actions would follow Murphy's rather cautious assessment.

The reluctance of Murphy and Deputy Commissioner Benjamin Ward, the highest-ranking black police official, to release further statements for several days reflected their apprehension that a replay of the Watts riots of 1965 would occur in Harlem in 1972. In addition, although the commissioner said the police "behaved with commendable restraint," he believed they were "poorly managed," having breached an agreement to treat mosques as "sensitive locations." This agreement banned police from "rushing into a mosque with guns." The commissioner, not wanting to publicly confirm that the NYPD had violated the agreement, minimized the importance of the police department's news releases, despite Daley's eagerness "to stage a big production number." Murphy was intent on not inflaming the situation, admitting, "We were caught, quite simply, on a tight-rope, and at a time when a bit of soft-shoe tiptoeing would have been prudent."[10]

Days later, the commanding officer of patrolman Cardillo's precinct, Deputy Inspector Jack Haugh, resigned from the department, criticizing Murphy for not defending his officers. Haugh explained, "I waited twenty-four hours after Cardillo died on Friday and again after his burial. No word came from headquarters. When Patrolman Cardillo was killed, he was doing his job properly. All we wanted was a clear, unequivocal statement . . . saying that he was in that mosque doing his job and doing it properly."[11]

Rashomon Reactions.   Clearly, two policing worlds had sharply clashed. Top police leadership was sensitive to the outside minority community; the rank and file were more attuned to the needs of their fellow officers.[12] Such "management-cop/street-cop" cleavage is not unusual. In this case, it was especially pronounced, provoking damning indictments of the city's police and political leadership.

What makes the mosque incident even more striking, however, is that the NYPD was eighteen months into its most ambitious reform campaign of the modern era. More effective management was its centerpiece, its all-purpose instrument, which, Murphy believed, should have helped the department avert such a situation—armed officers entering a mosque in violation of a standing order. The commissioner was subsequently candid: "Here I am admitting that even after eighteen months of reform . . . the department was still far from up to snuff. . . . [B]etter management . . . would have hammered this standing order home to the officers in every precinct where there was a mosque."[13]

Obviously, an ingredient that would enable management to "hammer this standing order home" was missing. What were the implications for the other reforms Murphy sought? How do organizational rifts and communications gaps affect attempts to change policing? While dramatic, this was not the first time reform and resistance would coexist uneasily. Their ebb and flow would be the backdrop for later changes as well.

Adaptive Superficial Change

In most large-city police departments, substantive reform has historically been the exception, rather than the rule. Most changes are surface adjustments to outside demands and pressures. This is reflected in the NYPD's early reform efforts, periodic corruption-control ventures, and recent emphases on community-oriented policing.

Early Reform Efforts.   The establishment of the NYPD in 1845 was influenced by its 1829 predecessor, the London Metropolitan Police. The founder of the London department, Sir Robert Peel, stressed that "the police are the public, and the public are the police." In New York City, the police provided commercial licensing, transient housing, and other services on behalf of local political leaders. Drawing on the London Metropolitan Police philosophy, the NYPD's first patrol guide proclaimed, "the prevention of crime being the most important object in your view, . . . the absence of crime will be considered the best proof of the efficiency of the police."[14] As will be seen, however, measures of crime prevention and recorded crime have rarely served management as benchmarks of police efficiency.

Until the 1890s, the NYPD had more in common with the police departments of other eastern industrial urban centers than with London's Metropolitan Police. The department's organization, management, recruitment, and promotion policies were enmeshed in the dealings of New York City's patronage-conscious politicos. Police corruption was viewed as part of the overall municipal corruption.

Beginning in the late nineteenth century, early reform efforts were therefore directed at disentangling the links between the police, vice industries, politicians, and gangs. In 1883, New York City's introduction of the written civil service examination was considered an important anti–political-machine model for the nation. The establishment of (supposedly) objective written merit standards was designed to distance police officers from corrupt politicians who appointed, promoted, and rewarded.[15]

In 1894, a coalition party of Republicans and anti-Tammany Democrats made a concerted attack on New York's corrupt political system by selecting Theodore Roosevelt as president of the Police Board of Commissioners. Pursuing organizational control, the board centralized authority so that commanders were made responsible to the department's chief executive rather than to the ward bosses. The ambitious attempt is noteworthy for its brief struggle and limited stamina. The formidable opposition of the liquor industry, fellow commissioners, and Boss Thomas Platt successfully obstructed Roosevelt's control over the police and hastened his departure. TR's influence was "more form than substance, and things soon returned to normal."[16]

Subsequent police reform efforts drew upon the Progressive Era's drive for greater efficiency through professional, scientific management. Despite the use of such Progressive-Era hallmarks as organizational division of labor, specialization, centralization, and expanded executive personnel and budgetary powers, many reforms had limited impact. Frequent turnover, for example, diminished the authority of any single police commissioner. When the third reform administration in twenty years emerged in 1914, it was clear that advocates for change had limited staying power: "Reform was not seen by many police as a good long-time prospect," wrote police expert Thomas Reppetto. "[C]ops who cooperated with them ended up in disfavor."[17]

Spurred by Mayor Fiorello LaGuardia and top police brass, the New York Police Department's reform efforts reemerged in the 1930s. In response to these efforts, however, officers distanced themselves from the perpetual contests between regulars and reformers. What began as a means of improving the functioning of the police transformed the NYPD into an insular, self-protective organization typified by a smooth but less creative routine. Structural change was wrought, but much of it led, unintentionally, to less effective crime control. Expanded centralization, rigidity, division, and stagnation nudged the NYPD into the "backwater of innovation in police administration."[18]

Combating Police Corruption. Corruption scandals within the NYPD have arisen with curious regularity, roughly every twenty years. These events attract everyone's attention, offer uncommon opportunities, and frequently galvanize action. Yet departmental responses, typically adaptive in nature, treat the symptoms, not the causes, and are rarely sustained.[19]

Since the 1890s, six commissions have been established to investigate specific instances of corruption within the NYPD. All commissions were formed hard on the heels of public cases of police turpitude. Recurrent themes thread through the scandals and their aftermaths. In 1895, the Lexow Commission uncovered corrupt Tammany–police liaisons, which included monthly payoffs from gamblers and brothel keepers, police extortion of legitimate businesses, voting interference, and assault on and harassment of immigrants. The initial fee for opening a brothel ranged from

$300 to $500; officers collected a monthly fee of $50 to $100.[20]

In July 1912, a gambler and informer named Herman "Beansey" Rosenthal was killed outside a Times Square hotel after providing information to the Manhattan district attorney about police payoffs. Convicted of the murder were Lieutenant Charles Becker, commander of a special squad that reported to the police commissioner's office, and four gunmen. Appointed that year, the Curran Committee exposed thriving corruption and graft infused with extensive extortion and blackmail. The committee recommended departmental reorganization, salary increases, improved training and recruitment, and better crime tracking and record keeping.

A third commission, the Seabury Commission of 1932, unearthed widespread corruption throughout the city's criminal justice system, including police extortion of money from innocent citizens and from prostitutes. This state commission exposed an intricate system of mobster payoffs to police and political officials. The commission's recommendations led to the appointment of Special Prosecutor Thomas Dewey, who successfully prosecuted corrupt police officers and organized crime luminaries, such as Lucky Luciano. Revelations of police bribes and connections with gamblers and bootleggers led to Mayor LaGuardia's appointment of a reform police commissioner, Lewis Valentine. The new commissioner purged some crooked officers but had limited impact on the department overall, despite his twelve-year tenure, the longest of any New York City police commissioner. Luciano, a rich, powerful mob boss, publicly mocked LaGuardia and Valentine's reform agenda: "We got all the rest—the D.A., the cops, everything."[21] The twin viruses of ingrained corruption and inbred political connections proved extremely resistant to inoculations of reform.

Eighteen years later, another scandal emerged when Harry Gross, an influential Brooklyn bookmaker, testified to a grand jury about far-reaching police gambling, bribery, and extortion operations. Gross affirmed in his 1950 deposition that he paid $1 million a year to police to protect his $20-million-a-year gambling operation. A five-year inquiry resulted in 300 resignations, 21 indictments, 10 convictions, and a request to the Institute of Public Administration for recommendations on upgrading the police department. The institute's report held that the "explosive issues" surrounding corruption were amenable to administrative control.[22] Once again, the NYPD responded with more training, specialized divisions, centralization, and command authority, as well as the introduction of investigation units. Despite this succession of four reform attempts, "none . . . succeeded in reforming the New York City Police Department on a lasting basis."[23]

The Knapp Commission

Fast-forward to 1970, when scandal—this time, police graft—again thrust the issue of police corruption onto center stage, and a chain of events starkly revealed the NYPD's instinctive defensive maneuvers. Initially, top police and city government officials were unresponsive to two of their own men—patrolman Frank Serpico and Detective David Durk—who had made allegations of police graft. Serpico and Durk then circumvented official channels and contacted the *New York Times*, which researched their claims. After six months of investigation, a three-part exposé of police corruption appeared in the *Times*. According to Robert Daley, the NYPD deputy commissioner for public information, "The project stayed secret. . . . But by late April, word of the imminent news story was all over town, and Mayor Lindsay, in the venerable tradition of public servants, announced the appointment of his own special committee [the Rankin Committee] to investigate police corruption. This would take

the sting out of the *Times* exposé when it finally appeared. The
mayor would be able to announce casually, 'Oh yes, we've already taken care of that.'"[24]

Lindsay's committee, named after its chairman, the city's corporation counsel, J. Lee Rankin, included Police Commissioner
Howard Leary, the commissioner of the New York City Department of Investigation, and the Manhattan and Bronx district attorneys. It was formed on April 23, 1970—one day before the
first of the *New York Times* articles. Three weeks later, the committee reported that this was "an undertaking of far greater magnitude than that originally envisioned." A thorough evaluation
required "a full-time investigative body with skilled full-time
staff." Having insufficient time and wanting to avoid the public's perception of conflicts of interest, the Rankin Committee
recommended disbanding.[25] In the skeptical words of Deputy Police Commissioner Daley, all committee members "owed primary political allegiance to the Lindsay administration, (and)
impressed nobody. . . . [The committee] voted itself out of existence, recommending that the Mayor appoint an 'independent'
commission to investigate alleged police corruption. His hand
forced, the Mayor now did so."[26]

"The Blue Wall of Silence."   Thus, the Knapp Commission,
named for its chairman, Whitman Knapp, came into existence
on May 21, 1970, a week after the disbanding of the short-lived
Rankin Committee. For several weeks, the commission strug-
gled against the resistance of the NYPD, especially in regard to
the commission's intention of recruiting undercover police to
catch corrupt cops. The *New York Times* reported on a tape-
recorded conversation that underscored this well-entrenched
resistance. A police officer had asked a "top uniformed police
official responsible for stamping out corruption" what his unit
had accomplished, and the assistant chief replied, "I think I have

done a damn good job of protecting the Commissioner against the onslaughts of outside agencies."[27]

Investigative research by the *Times* triggered a scorching and unrelenting series of headlines, stories, investigations, and a two-year Knapp Commission study. On the morning of April 25, 1970, two days after Mayor Lindsay's appointment of the Rankin Committee, the *Times* headlined a front-page story, "Graft Paid to Police Here Said to Run into Millions." The subtitle underlined departmental stratification and stagnation: "Some on force accuse officials of failure to act." The journalistic exposé recounted an organized system of payoffs from narcotics dealers, gamblers, and businessmen.[28] It was alleged that a number of high-ranking city administrators and NYPD officials had failed to investigate cases of corruption brought to their attention.

The Knapp Commission's August 1972 report struck familiar chords, confirming "widespread" corruption that centered on narcotics. In addition, it revealed that plainclothesmen assigned to enforce gambling laws had established regular payment procedures, called "pads," with gambling establishments. Corruption spilled over to include detective shakedowns (detectives getting money from store owners in exchange for extra police protection or protection from mob or gang activity) as well as payments to street patrolmen from construction sites, bars, and grocery stores.

The commission, aware of corruption's durability and cyclical patterns, lamented, "Investigations have occurred on the average of once in twenty years since before the turn of the century, and yet conditions exposed by one investigation seem substantially unchanged when the next one makes its report." Encouraged by the police department's most recent responses, however, the commission voiced cautious optimism: "A considerable momentum for reform has been generated, but not enough time has elapsed to reverse attitudes that have been solidifying for many years. . . . After previous investigations, the momentum was allowed to evaporate."[29]

The commission pointed to the "blue wall of silence" of the NYPD and defined two primary categories of corrupt officers, "meat eaters" and "grass eaters." Meat eaters, according to the commission, were officers who "aggressively misuse their police powers for personal gain. The grass eaters simply accept the payoffs that the happenstances of police work throw their way." Although the meat eaters got the attention of the press because of the larger payoffs, the grass eaters, being far more prevalent, represented a pervasive problem. Their larger numbers "tend to make corruption 'respectable,'"[30] promoting a code of silence toward wrongdoing. Violators of this code were considered traitors and put themselves in danger.

Murphy's Reforms

The Knapp Commission Report offered corrective proposals and reviewed the reforms of the new NYPD commissioner, Patrick V. Murphy, who replaced Leary soon after the commission's investigations began. Murphy considered himself a reform agent, and his house-cleaning agenda not only represented significant anti-corruption measures but also embodied a bid to recast the NYPD fundamentally. As in all major organizational overhauls, some of Murphy's innovations subsequently improved the department's performance, whereas other changes actually became impediments to later reform efforts.

Murphy believed the NYPD had long lain idle in the backwater of modern police management, and he seized the opportunity to strike a blow for police reform. Despite the sobering realization that the "whole police world would be watching," he embarked on a mission into uncharted territory in the face of enormous obstacles. Murphy noted that "a *real* program of reform had in fact never been tried in New York, indeed had barely been tried anywhere else in the entire United States because (a) few know how even to begin the effort and (b) few know beforehand how it might in the end work out."[31]

"In the Grip of Fear for a Year."   Key to Murphy's reform was command accountability. Previous crusades, dating to the 1890s, had advocated holding all commanders responsible by tightening the reins from the top. This commissioner took the principle one step further. Steeped in the literature of contemporary management principles, Murphy held supervisors' feet to the fire, insisting that commanders at all ranks be answerable for their actions and for those of their subordinates. This applied from "the lowest patrol officer to the highest ranking chiefs." Murphy wanted to break out from an NYPD history in which "responsibility and authority had been so dispersed . . . that whenever something went wrong, it was often difficult to determine who was to blame."[32]

More than just a sound management principle, Murphy's command accountability would, it was hoped, budge the department's institutional inertia. Murphy was critical of former Mayor Wagner's four lawyer–police commissioners, a succession of administrators who failed "to grasp the intricacies of managing a huge police bureaucracy. . . . Headquarters was not in control of the department."[33] This lack of control, Murphy believed, curbed his predecessors' capability to check corruption and advance real change.

How, then, does a new commissioner expel organizational stagnation, introduce accountability, and wield managerial control? Murphy's approach was to act decisively but with deliberation, not showing his hand too quickly. Known for his quiet but forceful style in previous positions (including head of the Syracuse, Washington, and Detroit police departments), Murphy proceeded to amass power.

Intent on building public support, the new commissioner used every opportunity to proclaim his reform message. Murphy, like many power brokers, understood public perception to be intimately coupled with the exercise of power. The new police head must not only be cognizant of the tools necessary to influence decisions, but also be perceived as adept at using them.

Although appointed for a fixed term, the New York police commissioner essentially serves at the mayor's discretion. Lose the mayor's confidence, and the commissioner is gone. A further complication is the involvement of the mayor in the department's affairs and the extent to which he will take credit for NYPD policy and personnel decisions. This issue was very much in evidence in the NYPD of the mid-1990s, the era of Mayor Giuliani and his conspicuous Commissioner Bratton.

The police commissioner has formal authority to appoint senior officials above the rank of captain. Some 180 positions were above that rank in 1970. Appointing one's own top-level personnel is crucial to introducing reform and, in the view of many innovators, sends a message to lower ranks.

Murphy was intent on using his power of appointment to win the force's allegiance. He prophetically proclaimed, "A new police administrator's immediate task is to identify that [upper level] faction which to the younger, more idealistic, more potentially productive officers in the ranks below appears to include the good guys frozen out of the very top positions by the old guard clique. . . . The administrator must selectively but rapidly begin to move its members up at the expense of the bad clique currently in power."[34] Murphy's zealous cleansing of the NYPD top-level management presaged Bratton's 1994 vow to purge the department's high-level "dead wood."

Murphy systematically and "selectively" replaced the old guard with those more sympathetic to his policies. However, one must question the slow and deliberate pace of the commissioner's departmental replacements. Key personnel changes took place in stages. Murphy started with the two top positions, then waited for a while before moving to the next levels of "super chiefs" and assistant chiefs. These personnel were removed one at a time, sometimes at intervals of a month or more. This informed but deliberate pace had the advantage of providing time to assess incumbents, but that may have been the only advantage. At the end of six months, although many of former police commissioner Leary's top people had been replaced, some still remained.

Discussing his first major personnel undertaking—replacing First Deputy Commissioner John Walsh, the powerful incumbent in the department's second most important position—Murphy moved behind the scenes to "topple Walsh without an unseemly show of power."[35] A concern to avoid an "unseemly" display of power was typical of Murphy's style. But was this approach preferable to moving all at once and making a clean administrative sweep? What was viewed by Murphy as a subtle exercise of power that would leave his organization less shell-shocked actually had just the opposite effect. To those less sympathetic to Murphy: "He was very crafty and very slow, and this seemed to earn him more resentment than he had bargained for. Instead of a quick purge followed by calmness and jokes, headquarters was in the grip of fear for a year. . . . Murphy kept telling his commanders that he was forcing authority downward, but as they saw it he was merely waiting for them to make a decisive move, any sort of move, so as to have grounds for forcing them to retire."[36]

Some observers, more appreciative of the multiple obstacles and uncertainties confronting the new commissioner, have kinder things to say. One former city official commented sympathetically, "Murphy's job was to turn the department around and restore public confidence before it was irretrievably lost. . . . [T]he city's five district attorneys had already said that they couldn't do the job, and the police unions had declared they wouldn't permit drastic changes in established procedures. So the new commissioner had to . . . shake up the department from within without cracking the pillars of the structure."[37]

But shouldn't the "pillars of the structure" be cracked—even at a cost—if one wishes to introduce fundamental change? Consider what is lost by not cracking these pillars. In a polyglot, geographically dispersed environment like New York City, top-level police officials are often closely allied with a diversity of other community leaders and groups. Political connections still count. Allowed to remain in office under such circumstances, undesirable administrators may increasingly rely on their outside supporters and become more firmly dug in. These are the ways of a large, urban police department and realistically, they must be taken into account.[38]

What message do the rank and file hear when personnel changes are uncertain or pending? Is a new direction clearly planted in their minds? The troops are skeptical of high-level communiqués delivered in the field. Instead, a wait-and-see attitude serves them well. As if confronted by a violent storm, those in the organization's "basement" usually survive longer than those higher up, particularly NYPD commissioners, whose average tenure is about two and a half years. Murphy claimed that the executive corps knew he meant business since the turnover rate was over 90 percent by the end of his administration, but he misses the point. Every commissioner has a limited window of opportunity for programmatic change. In addition, few know when a commissioner will depart, regardless of his clear policy positions. This may be even more pronounced with a commissioner like Murphy, who moved frequently from department to department and was viewed as closely hitched to City Hall. As we shall see, the 1994 reform period ushered in an alternative approach to power transformation.

Corruption Reforms.   Personnel matters aside, Murphy's priority was the pressing corruption issue, which was prominently featured in the news while the Knapp Commission and a state investigation panel peered over his shoulder. The new commissioner diagnosed the disease and performed radical surgery.

Command accountability and organizational reshuffling continue to be the ingredients of police reform. Murphy looked on the department's former supervisory procedures with skepticism, believing they fostered corrupt behavior since cops "were not fundamentally or irremediably corrupt."[39] Under the new commissioner's regime, supervisors were now personally accountable for misconduct in their units. All commanders were required to prepare periodic reports detailing corruption opportunities and plans for their reduction.[40] Soon many supervisors were moved, and hundreds of plainclothes officers were demoted or transferred.

Carving out a new anticorruption structure, Murphy redesigned the Internal Affairs Division (IAD) and doubled the number of internal investigation officers in order to actively ferret out field misconduct. The commissioner also curtailed corruption opportunities, targeting the poorly managed Detective Bureau and its Narcotics Division, "a viper's nest of corruption of the worst kind."[41] Murphy moved the detectives from their precinct bases so they would no longer enjoy a monopoly of contacts with merchants, thus reducing the detectives' opportunities to offer protective services in exchange for graft. Murphy further experimented with some larger detective areas, called districts, which were the size of several precincts. Under the "cover" of increased specialization, districts were broken down into separate units—homicide and assault, robbery, and burglary and larceny. However, this attempt to expand the detectives' geographic areas and limit close community contact did not survive beyond Murphy's administration.

The reform commissioner's reorganization did not stop there. Murphy moved the Narcotics Division from the Detective Bureau into a newly created Organized Crime Control Bureau

(OCCB). This move gave the commissioner more opportunities to limit the temptations of narcotics officers, since the OCCB head reported directly to one of the commissioner's top aides. This change basically stands today. In addition, Murphy consolidated all other plainclothesmen into OCCB, including the plainclothes gambling squads, which had been in the patrol boroughs and divisions. Later commissioners reversed that trend.

Applauding Murphy's reform agenda, the Knapp Commission urged the department to go even further.[42] Similarly, it cautioned that "it is still too early to determine if the many changes instituted to improve accountability will indeed force officers to act against corruption they know about. Continued monitoring will be necessary to determine if these programs are effective over the long run."[43]

The commission went beyond merely commenting on Murphy's reforms and making numerous pro forma recommendations.[44] It also pressed for an outside independent body with authority to prosecute corruption throughout the criminal justice system. This recommendation, based on the belief that the public and the police require an institution they can trust, resulted in a very active State Office of the Special Prosecutor for Corruption, which had jurisdiction over improper behavior or corruption in all criminal justice agencies in New York City. This office was disbanded in 1990 with the assurance that its $3 million budget would be transferred to New York City's five district attorneys. Illustrating the transitory nature of reform once the spotlight was off corruption, the redistribution of funds never happened, thus dealing the reform cause another blow.

Other Reforms.   While his highly visible attacks on corruption were receiving most of the public's attention, Commissioner Murphy updated behind-the-scenes crime reduction practices. These ventures, although introduced less systematically than the anticorruption measures, presaged 1990s managerial reforms.

"We were way behind in crime analysis and computerization," Murphy recalled years later. To correct this problem, each precinct selected a sergeant as a planning officer. The officer would receive a police academy crash course in analyzing statistics in order to plot and anticipate crime patterns. Murphy also grasped the need for smarter deployment. When not enforcing the law, patrol officers were to collect and analyze crime information. Tracking down repeat offenders required, Murphy believed, greater cooperation with probation, parole, and district attorneys. Years later, with more adequate funding, these proposals blossomed (see Chapter 5).

Murphy's administration advocated closer police ties to the community. Shortly after an outbreak of street disorders in the summer of 1971, the "Cop of the Block" program began in a corner of Brooklyn's Bedford-Stuyvesant area. Having been advised to get to know the business people and residents on their beat, each of the 110 officers of the 81st Precinct was expected to become familiar with the people on one or two of the precinct's 130 blocks. They were told to "rap with the people and make friends."[45] Twenty years later, Commissioner Lee P. Brown announced a "pilot project" in two precincts entitled the "Cop's Block" program. Although the new project was not named after its precursor, the aim of "making personal contact with residents and merchants on their assigned blocks" clearly paralleled 1971. Murphy himself considers the "Cop of the Block" program a legacy. "We rooted the idea in enough precincts to build sufficient resident support to prevent its abandonment during the fiscal crunch [of the mid-1970s]," he says.

On the other hand, Murphy's 1971 inauguration of team policing, known as Neighborhood Police Teams (NPTs), vividly captured both the promise and disappointment of fundamental reform. What started out as a "major innovation" and alternative to the existing patrol structure was alternately absorbed and resisted by that organization.[46]

The department decentralized certain patrol units as NPTs in order to build closer community bonds and fight crime. Responsible for all police activities within their sectors, these NPTs supplemented rather than supplanted existing patrol deployment, foreshadowing today's community policing. This arrangement triggered resistance from the existing command structure and sealed the teams' fate. Gradual abandonment followed inadequate planning and implementation, insufficient attention to obstacles, and rapid expansion of teams in response to constituent pressures. No department mechanism was in place to oversee this innovation, and before long team members were reduced to relaying community complaints to an unreceptive hierarchy.

Conclusion: Murphy's Lessons

Patrick Murphy entered office with considerable advantages. A reformer by nature, he adroitly used the pressure of an investigative commission and a recent corruption scandal to navigate turbulent political waters. He was armed with encyclopedic knowledge that came from being a former NYPD official, an experienced police administrator, and a student of contemporary management and police history.

The commissioner knew that historically, opportunities for fundamental NYPD change were limited. His 1970–1973 stewardship nevertheless represents a major innovative period in NYPD modern reform. "To make an impact," he told one of his key supporters, "go where the fire is."[47] By all accounts, his impact on corruption was significant. Barbara Gelb, having studied the NYPD from 1972 to 1982, concluded, "In the ten years, it evolved from one of the most corrupt and brutal into one of the cleanest and most judicious."[48]

Murphy imaginatively laid the groundwork for anchoring police work to more intelligent and productive use of time—issues that flourished in the 1990s (see Chapters 4–8). Few commis-

sioners have tried to do so much; few have evoked so many reactions. Some critics complain that restraining officers was the
leitmotif of his reforms. The implication was that "the police
officers, like children, had to be kept out of places where they
might get in trouble."[49]

This critique falls short; it is easy to second-guess gutsy leaders. In addition, the criticism ignores many of Murphy's anticorruption advances, which penetratingly examined organization
and management arrangements. The commissioner not only was
attentive to crime analysis and community-type policing, he focused on police career paths. He recognized the effectiveness of
plainclothes units, which also opened up a whole new career
path for young officers. One high-ranking official, who launched
his career in plainclothes, recalls rookie police reactions to the
commissioner: "Murphy made his presence known; that was unusual for a police commissioner."

Murphy's administration also demonstrates that the NYPD is
like a massive ocean liner—its course is extremely difficult to
change. A reluctant crew savors management obstacles, pleased
with the inefficiencies of an enormous bureaucracy. Effective reform requires more than confronting structural and management resistance. Concepts of leadership and command accountability must transcend slogans and must be recast in operational
practices. Moreover, mechanisms must be in place to ensure
their regularity.

Murphy's record graphically portrays the police department's
broad institutional capacity to either block or absorb reform. His
tenure provides several lessons: First, despite powerful political
pressures, fundamental recasting did not come easily, even for a
commissioner who relished the role of administrator. Notwith-
standing the sympathy and loyalty of hand-picked top-level personnel, the department skillfully engulfed some of Murphy's
changes without disturbing many existing practices.

Second, the strategy of a staggered policy and personnel overhaul, on a top-down basis, tended to minimize the engagement of many street-level cops, who considered themselves organizational orphans. Gelb, a strong Murphy supporter, reports on the "schism that Murphy unavoidably left as his legacy to the department, along with his reforms. The top brass was divided between the two factions: the traditionalists . . . (their credo was: We've always done it this way and it works, change for change's sake can be dangerous) and the innovators, the now leaderless opposition who, in the Murphy image, collected what they believed to be scientific data and recommended change."[50] Murphy swept out the department, but not entirely.

Third, and quite important, the reformers of the 1970s were preoccupied with corruption. Thus, for example, precinct and other commanders were, more than ever, held responsible for their commands and their subordinates' behaviors. Although this principle was meant to apply to all precinct activities, corruption was the major operational concern. Given the corruption-prone political climate of the 1970s and 1980s, it was understandable that corruption was first and foremost on every commander's mind. Former and current police officials who served as precinct commanders during that period repeatedly cite corruption control and peaceful community relations as major preoccupations. Precinct heads were aware that they could lose their commands if corruption emerged. Crime control, on the other hand, was only a blip on the NYPD radar screen.

This preoccupation with corruption makes sense from another perspective as well. The commissioner subscribed to the prevailing academic and police wisdom that crime was the product of a host of social and economic factors including "overpopulation, underemployment, ill housed and poorly integrated cities . . . youth unemployment, cultural anomie, family disintegration, alcoholism, mental health breakdown, racism, and child neglect." These factors outweighed police efforts, since "very little of what we did had an intimate connection to crime or crime prevention." Therefore, it made far more sense to focus on corruption, which was well within the commissioner's "reach and grasp," as opposed to crimes that were "not within his control."[51]

Murphy proved that reform requires constant attention, a lesson that not all of his successors observed. Despite the intensity of Murphy's anticorruption efforts and their solid impacts, deep-rooted issues related to corruption did not go quietly into the night. Many hibernated, only to resurface later in an altered state. An informed scholar's 1978 analysis concluded that the "scandal and reform . . . had reduced police corruption to a very minimal level. Six years after the Knapp Commission hearings, corruption no longer appears to be widespread."[52] Fourteen years later, however, another wave of scandals exposed corruption that was far more serious and damaging than the 1970 NYPD scandal. We will look at the scandals and reforms of this period (1984–1994) next.

THE NYPD
1984–1994

On October 29, 1984, police officers attempted to carry out an order to evict Eleanor Bumpurs—an elderly, emotionally disturbed black woman—from her apartment in a Bronx housing development. In the ensuing struggle, Mrs. Bumpurs was killed by Officer Stephen Sullivan, who shot her twice with a shotgun when she attacked officers with a kitchen knife. Officer Sullivan was subsequently acquitted of all criminal charges. Nevertheless (and perhaps predictably), the incident intensified accusations of police racism, voiced during congressional hearings convened in Harlem to investigate allegations of NYPD brutality.

Five months later, in March 1985, a car driven by Sergeant Frederick Sherman, who was accompanied by two other on-duty police officers, struck two pedestrians on Park Avenue, killing Dr. Hyman Chernow. According to a departmental investigation, the officers left the scene of the accident, and two of the officers falsified police records to cover up the accident. Sherman was convicted of manslaughter, and the other two officers were found guilty of lesser charges.

Departmental records revealed that Sherman's application to join the NYPD had twice been denied on the basis of psychiatric findings, only to be reversed on an appeal to the Civil Service

Commission. At one point during his eleven years with the department, he had pleaded no contest to drunken driving charges, for which he was fined twenty-five vacation days and ordered to undergo alcohol counseling. He was subsequently promoted to sergeant on the basis of his civil service examination.

One month later, a sergeant and an officer in the 106th Precinct in Queens were arrested after an alleged drug dealer accused them of torturing him with an electric stun gun. Investigations revealed high-ranking knowledge of similar incidents. The cases resulted in indictments, dismissals, and the removal of twenty-five individuals, including some top Queens borough commanders. Commissioner Benjamin Ward publicly rebuked top officials for allowing this type of behavior to continue unchecked. In May, Mayor Edward Koch, in response to mounting pressures, appointed an advisory committee to assess a wide spectrum of NYPD management and personnel practices.[1]

Professionalism and Performance

These three incidents, occurring within six months, brought into question the NYPD's ability to perform competently. Consequently, the mayoral panel (named the Zuccotti Committee after its chairman, John Zuccotti) was given a broad mandate to examine the department's procedures for recruitment, selection, training, assessment, promotion, supervision, and management. The committee's authority sharply contrasted with that given to previous commissions, whose mandates were limited to single issues, primarily corruption.

The Zuccotti Committee's multiple assignments reflected more than just the political fallout from recent events. The origins of police reform are typically complex. This was especially true of the period from 1984 to 1994, when corruption and misconduct reemerged. During this time, the public's reactions to the police were still colored by events from the 1960s. The violence connected with the Civil Rights movement, and the urban

disturbances of that era, often ignited by seemingly routine encounters between white officers and minority citizens, spurred a
long period of inquiry (including two presidential commissions)
into police behavior. Such issues as police isolation from the
community, low minority representation on the force, and ineffective crime fighting became publicly linked to police brutality
and corruption. As a Joint New York State Legislative Committee on Crime put it, "[G]hetto residents are perfectly aware of the
corrupt relationship between racketeers and certain elements of
the Police Department, and for this reason, have a deep cynicism
concerning the integrity of the police in maintaining law and order in the community." [2]

Although these nationwide social forces influenced the
NYPD's 1984–1994 reform debates, their impact was remarkably blunted when they struck against the institutional granite
of the NYPD. Report after report and analysis after analysis ran
up against the same NYPD cultural-structural core resistance. In
1987, the Zuccotti Committee reported the findings of its long,
hard look.

The Zuccotti Committee

In the committee's view, professional police performance was
hobbled by an inflexible and outdated centralized bureaucracy.
Having expertly analyzed modern personnel and managerial options, the committee recommended upgrading and redesigning
selection, promotion, assessment, and management processes.
The end result would be a workforce more representative of, and
responsive to, the community.

Many of the committee's proposals, however, were seen by insiders as fundamental assaults on existing procedures, including
the tradition-bound civil service system, and accordingly, they
were fiercely resisted. The few recommendations adopted by the
NYPD were primarily easy add-ons (sometimes after a few mod-
ifications), which produced minimal waves to upset the status

quo of the department and police union. For example, a proposal for a research-based command college, affiliated with the City University of New York, was to provide executives with a "structured management training program." The proposal was watered down and became a series of seminars at the Police Management Institute, under the aegis of Columbia University.

The committee probed deeply into the cops' work setting and found that officers were generally poorly supervised, isolated, and detached from the community. This "supervisory crisis," it believed, was rooted in unfilled vacancies in sergeants' and lieutenants' positions, ineffective performance evaluations, and inadequate training. The committee also prescribed traditional remedies rarely taken seriously by ailing bureaucracies: enhanced command supervision and accountability. One could almost hear an echo from the 1972 Knapp Commission's report: "[T]he department's most fundamental managerial defect . . . [is] the utter failure to hold supervisors and commanders accountable for derelictions of their subordinates. . . . The pervasive failure . . . despite the efforts of some police commissioners . . . [in] translating dogma into operating routine."[3]

On the other hand, the Zuccotti Committee was encouraged by two crucial developments: the department's anticorruption efforts and the Community Patrol Officer Program (CPOP). The latter innovation was designed to promote joint police and community crime prevention. Unfortunately, the committee's views of both reform measures proved overly sanguine.

Clockwork Corruption

The Zuccotti Committee was neither designed for, nor immersed in, the ferreting out of corruption. The panel prophetically warned about rises in "drug related misconduct," which did not yet constitute a problem of "epidemic" proportions.[4]

The committee expressed confidence in the department's anticorruption procedures, based on the NYPD's handling of a major scandal in Brooklyn's Bedford-Stuyvesant area in 1986. The 77th Precinct officers, known as the "Buddy Boys," knocked down doors, stole money and drugs from dealers, and then resold the stolen drugs. The investigation of this case—the department's first major corruption scandal since the Knapp era—seemed to contrast significantly with "the unhappy events of the past." The investigation was conducted by the NYPD Internal Affairs Division, "an institutional legacy" of the Knapp Commission. According to Dr. Joseph Viteritti, the Zuccotti Committee's executive director, in the 1986 investigation, "the evidence pointed to the fact that the Department hierarchy was deeply engaged in exposing the wrongdoing rather than concealing it."[5]

The 1992 Drug Scandal.   While quite accurate in 1987, this view rang hollow five years later, when a corruption scandal again took center stage. In May 1992, Officer Michael Dowd of Brooklyn's 94th Precinct was arrested by Long Island's Suffolk County police for drug trafficking between Brooklyn bodegas (Hispanic-American grocery stores) and Long Island bars. At the time, Dowd was carrying eight ounces of cocaine. Additional cocaine was found in his police locker, and $20,000 in cash in his home. He frequently received $5,000 to $10,000 in payoffs from drug dealers in exchange for warning them about imminent police raids and the presence of federal agents. He also helped Dominican cocaine gangs with their drug deals by providing them with guns, badges, and police radios, and assisting in at least one murder.

On the eve of the appointment of yet another mayoral blue-ribbon panel, the Mollen Commission,[6] the chief of NYPD's Internal Affairs Division (IAD) acknowledged that the opportunities for drug-related corruption were unlimited, unprecedented, and extremely difficult to control: "There has never been a time in this job when we've been presented with more corruption hazards . . . [and] opportunity to make so much money so easily, so fast, and so undetected. . . . Recently two patrol officers found $325,000 in drug money in a car. . . . It's mind boggling; you can't even believe this."[7]

As vast as the opportunities for drug corruption were and as difficult as they were to monitor, the NYPD, according to the Mollen Commission, deliberately and repeatedly looked the other way when the corrupt activities of Dowd and other officers were brought to light.

Why this malignant neglect? The answer may be rooted in the late 1980s. What appeared to reformers to be a successful episode of institutional rehabilitation may have spelled disaster for that very organization. The 1986 drug scandal in the 77th Precinct had been unearthed by the department's own IAD, evoking the Zuccotti Committee's praise for its diligence. Yet the scandal's resulting twelve arrests, twenty-seven supervisory transfers, and one suicide were devastating to the institution and individual careers. The lesson for the NYPD: "If it ain't public, don't fix it," and when in doubt, sidestep scandal. So beginning in the fall of 1986, according to the Mollen Commission, "even corruption investigators understood that avoiding scandal was often more important than uncovering corruption. . . . This attitude began at the top."[8]

Sergeant Joseph Trimboli worked for a field unit of the post-Knapp IAD, helping to weed out borough- and precinct-level corruption. The fact that Trimboli's information on Dowd and requests for funding and equipment for tracking him were repeatedly rebuffed by his headquarters superiors led one top-level police official to conclude, "Trimboli proves that the post-Knapp safeguards don't work. The whole system has to be overhauled."[9]

Departmental Responses

From the moment Officer Dowd was arrested, the NYPD responded predictably with four highly defensive postures. Stage one was denial: "The problem is minimal." Dowd was said to represent a handful of rogue cops, enticed by drug trade opportunities, but checked, according to Commissioner Lee Brown, by the NYPD's anticorruption "system that police agencies across the country look to."[10]

Stage two was damage control: "We are looking into it." This followed press accounts that the department had hampered previous investigations of Dowd. Commissioner Brown responded by appointing his first deputy commissioner, Raymond Kelly, to supersede the chief of Inspection Services, Robert Beatty, who had been overseeing the investigation. The commissioner's new appointee "demonstrated heightened concern about how department corruption is examined and how that examination is being perceived."[11]

Stage three downplayed the need for an outside review commission: "We are doing something about it." Commissioner Brown unveiled a new anticorruption effort, the Critical Analysis and Response Program, under which any officer receiving five allegations of corruption or serious misconduct would be tagged and investigated. Also, the addition of twenty-three "highly qualified" investigators to the IAD staff, it was suggested, would remedy all problems: "Perhaps we didn't put enough efforts into Dowd individually," Chief Beatty said. "As allegation after allegation came in, they should have sent up a red flag and we should have gone after him full tilt. Now we'll have enough manpower to do it."[12] One reviewer described these moves for what they were, just empty motions. The NYPD was interested in the "tweaking and honing of existing mechanisms rather than replacing them."[13]

The fourth stage, desperate action, was instigated by police when the previous three responses failed to dampen criticism and thwart the appointment of an outside review body. The implied message was: "We are doing something dramatic about it." The Mollen Commission, appointed in July 1992, began its widely publicized hearings in late September the following year. Less than two months later, hoping to stave off more drastic, externally imposed transformations, a new police commissioner, Raymond Kelly, proudly announced his own changes in the NYPD's corruption-fighting apparatus: "The very structure that so brilliantly protected this department from corruption has become unbalanced and in need of significant change. It is time to retool for the 1990s."[14] The "significant change" was the elevation of IAD to full bureau status, reporting directly to the commissioner. The expanded bureau would consolidate several anticorruption units and replace field units with superior investigative teams supplied with better surveillance equipment. But this change satisfied the Mollen Commission no more than former Commissioner Murphy's anticorruption reforms twenty years earlier had fully satisfied the Knapp Commission. Both commissions called for outside anticorruption bodies independent of the NYPD.

Corruption Redux

Corruption, said the Mollen Commission, though less systemic than during the Knapp Commission period, had become more "serious and damaging." Renegade cops did more than just look the other way, participate in a "pad," or allow drug dealers to operate. These self-contained cells of corruption actively worked with criminals, had become dealers themselves, protected large drug rings, and helped them operate. Dowd, for example, earned $8,000 a week selling drugs and protecting drug dealers. One officer, known as "The Mechanic," enforced his street domain by brutally "tuning up," or hitting, citizens with lead-lined gloves.[15]

Although the Mollen and Knapp Commissions uncovered different varieties of corruption, both gauged it similarly. They underscored the police culture of silence, scandal-avoidance, mutual protection, and a distant, often hostile, "we versus they" mindset of the NYPD.

Nor had the issue of effective supervision paled. Knapp's finding of a "pervasive failure" to hold commanders responsible for subordinates' actions may have been repaired at one time, but it was surely broken now. The NYPD's "centerpiece and commitment" to maintain integrity, made during Commissioner Murphy's tenure, "eventually eroded because no mechanism was ever implemented to sustain it."[16]

The absence of anticorruption mechanisms did not prevent official expressions of "shock" when glitches were uncovered. In December 1986, the NYPD divulged findings from a survey: apparently, many sergeants and lieutenants did not know the names of the officers they supervised. Such an atmosphere of anonymity could effectively cripple corruption control. According to one department official, "probably the most horrendous" finding was that precinct commanding officers, required since the Murphy era to submit corruption hazard reports, had not generally discussed those reports with their sergeants and lieutenants, who were "the very people who have to control these corruption hazards."[17] Officialdom disclosed what all "nonofficialdom" already knew.

Lessons Learned

Extending command accountability into the heart of an organization is a formidable task. If there is to be a public unveiling, it should be the beginning of the story, not at the end. And resources, training, proper assignments and placement, and sufficient authority must provide the narrative. Ultimately, fundamental change requires a vibrant implementation plan, strategy, management approach, and, above all, constant monitoring. For the NYPD, this entails a radically different method of change from the top-down tactics traditionally embraced by such quasi-military institutions as police departments. Taking action, according to management guru E. Edward Deming, requires explaining "to a critical mass of people in the company why change is necessary and that the change will involve everybody. Enough people in the company must understand the . . . obstacles [and] what to do and how to do it."[18]

In the absence of such profound measures, reform efforts fall short, resulting in the same problems that plague most "management cop" innovations imposed on "street cop" culture. Like new automobile models, police projects "wow the heck out of the public in test marketing, and the models are rushed into mass production . . . on the same assembly line that produced the Edsel. The end result is not a Cadillac or even a new car, but the same old Edsel with a Cadillac hood ornament slapped on it."[19]

Doomsday prophecies of abortive changes can be self-fulfilling. Real command accountability, whether focused on corruption or crime fighting, requires reconstruction. The New York Police Department's IAD had not just broken down; it was ill-prepared to anticipate changing corruption opportunities. The NYPD was not a "learning organization" proactively searching for fundamental improvement. Change was unplanned and adaptive— designed to deflect external pressures. So whereas the Mollen Commission's observations were particularly trenchant with respect to recruitment, selection, in-service training, strengthened intelligence-gathering units, and promotion polices, they essentially were drawn from the same well that supplied previous reform analyses. No doubt their proposals, such as a permanent outside body to assess the department's anticorruption efforts, would have helped immeasurably. In a turbulent urban world, however, with multiple demands on and expectations of the police, would these reforms be enough? Not when they failed to speak specifically to "a critical mass," steadfast implementation, and monitoring mechanisms.

NYPD Community Policing Reforms

New York's corruption scandals diminished community trust, and they also threatened to stymie the NYPD's major efforts to involve residents as crime-fighting partners. Community policing held lofty aspirations but encountered many barriers.

High Expectations Encounter Ground-Level Problems.   As noted in Chapter 1, community policing is a profound shift from traditional law enforcement—with its aloof, patrol-car responses to crime incidents—to a new model that embraces ground-level crime prevention and fear reduction through joint police-community problem solving.[20] Community policing "pushes the envelope" for a large, urban police force. Nevertheless, the NYPD took on the challenge in July 1984, when it introduced the Community Patrol Officer Program (CPOP) as a pilot project in a single precinct. Reminiscent of Commissioner Murphy's 1970s "Cop on the Block" program, CPOP was designed to operate as a distinct unit of community patrol officers (CPOs), with a supervising sergeant reporting directly to the precinct commander. Each CPO had primary responsibility for addressing crime and order maintenance problems within his or her permanently assigned beat.

While noting some exciting CPOP capabilities, an in-depth study of the program between December 1986 and February 1988, when the CPOP was expanding, reported familiar NYPD hurdles. For example, the study noted that whereas community policing "represents a potential paradigm shift in the organization and delivery of police services . . . the transformation will require some dramatic changes in the basic organization and management of police services."[21] There was much to overcome. Ironically, in dealing with the public, CPOs utilized law enforcement techniques more often than did regular motor patrols. CPOs faced daunting tasks: They found it difficult to mobilize citizen participation where none already existed, and lost opportunities to solve problems that were at the root of many disturbances.

Making CPOP "structures and processes work [was] an uncertain and difficult task;"[22] it required gaining the acceptance of the entire organization, including the cooperation of other NYPD units. One researcher saw traditional patrol officers ridiculing CPOs as privileged social workers, detached from the department's daily crime-fighting pressures. CPOP officers were unflatteringly known as C"MOM"s and "the untouchables."[23] Tensions and resentments arise when separate branches, such as the CPOP, are viewed as favored elites absorbed in an alien method of policing. In the absence of solid implementation, organizational units divide into hostile camps.[24]

Higher Expectations Meet Deeper Problems.   Despite CPOP's shaky foundation, later reforms built upon that program. By 1990 community policing, no longer restricted to a select number of officers, grew to involve the whole department, "patrol as well as specialized units, civilian as well as uniformed employees."[25] Mayor David Dinkins and Police Commissioner Lee Brown heralded NYPD's 1991 "transformation." This change, however, was based on a sweeping, in-depth study of the department's staffing needs and resources by "panels of senior executive staff."[26] Once again, change was implemented in a traditional, top-down approach.

Representing the department's "dominant operational philosophy," the CPOP was awarded a notably large expansion of personnel, from 786 to 4,895—an increase of 523 percent. Newly hired and existing officers, freed from radio patrol, served in ten-member community patrol–problem solving teams, which were deployed first in a model precinct and eventually expanded to all precincts by 1994.

The NYPD plan received high marks. One report termed it a "triumph, probably the most detailed analysis of the department's staffing needs in its 145-year history."[27] Dr. Thomas Reppetto, the head of the Citizens Crime Commission, a private watchdog group, said, "I've read every anti-crime plan put out since the 19th century, and this is the most impressive. This could well be a historic moment for the city."[28] Not surprisingly, the ambitious community-policing design was, like most police plans, prodded by outside events. In 1990, gang activity, drug violence, and random shootings continued to trouble many New York neighborhoods. And the summer's fatal stabbing of a Utah tourist protecting his mother from a subway mugger provoked a storm of national publicity, outrage, and editorials declaring the city's crime out of control.

The 1990 NYPD self-study provided the foundation for the department's widely publicized community-policing blueprint of 1991.[29] This document projected that community-policing values would surmount the resistance of the department's "traditional paramilitary . . . central control over most activities . . . [and] independent thought." The blueprint prescribed anti-bureaucratic remedies: "risk taking, innovative thinking . . . a tightened organization with a minimum of layers . . . [and] a management capability for direction and oversight of a highly decentralized policing."[30] Major streamlining of this magnitude is a tall order. One commentator saw NYPD's potential as "the nation's largest use of the new philosophy."[31] Commissioner Brown labeled the plan "revolutionary," but the changes were "evolutionary because they will take time to achieve."[32] Herein lies the problem. How much time would be required, and how much time was available?

Taking Time. A commissioner's window of opportunity is typically limited, especially given the average tenure of just a little more than two years. For Commissioner Brown, events conspired to make his timetable even more compressed. Although he became commissioner in January 1990, it was another full year before he unveiled his new approach to policing. Furthermore, Brown eventually resigned for personal reasons twenty months after the announcement of his revolutionary proposal. Three months before Brown's resignation, Officer Dowd was arrested on Long Island for drug trafficking, arousing an all-consuming series of newspapers accounts, scandals, and Mollen Commission hearings. In effect, Brown really had less time than most commissioners to get his reforms off the ground. How careful was the planning and implementation? Not very, it turned out.

While cognizant of the scale of the undertaking, the 1991 blueprint did not take advantage of the knowledge gained from CPOP predecessors or comparable efforts in other jurisdictions. With the help of outside consultants, the NYPD's top echelon crafted the new policing strategy during a brief period. Sustaining the street cops' traditional "wait-and-see" attitude toward innovation, the blueprint's designers never fully engaged critical masses of the police force. One officer noted in 1992, a year after NYPD's new policy was quietly put into effect, that he was unaware of community policing and was convinced that most of his fellow street cops and the community were in the same state of ignorance. In a conversation with the author, the officer explained, "You can't gain support for something we and the community know nothing about. I know the NYPD states that community policing is still in the infant stage, but even a mother brings her infant into the park to show off to her friends. She tells them how much he weighs, how tall, how long the labor was, and so forth. Communication begins with her friends, and soon every mother in the park is talking about babies. Community policing hasn't done this."

Implementation of the new policy was an afterthought. The plan included a section titled "Chronological Listing of Community Policing Tasks. Command Responsibility," which was merely a listing of tasks and the offices with primary and secondary responsibilities. Missing were a chronology and time-tables with stated deadlines for completed tasks. Many of the tasks were bewildering and vague. The entirety of Task Sixteen, for example, was to: "Initiate a Committee on Community Policing Implementation. Responsibilities: First Deputy Commissioner." One would think that this task would already have been completed or at least head the list of assignments.

After the blueprint was released in January 1991, the next official reference to implementation occurred a month later, when the commissioner announced a forthcoming reorganization plan "setting forth a 'road map' for the switch to community policing."[33] The road map quickly faded. Instead, one heard this frequently uttered imperative: "The train is in the station, and you had better get aboard"—hardly an invitation that would foster commitment. Police may recognize the train, feel they have been on it before, think it is going the wrong way, or be unsure the tracks are straight. In this instance, in the absence of a shared, organizationwide vision, they saw their future linked with the reliable bureaucratic train, not with the top cop's community-policing train. There would be other organizational trains, they were sure.

In April 1991, the NYPD issued "Department Priorities 1991," which listed ten priorities. Perhaps not surprising to many, within just three months, community policing had slipped into fourth place—to "Strengthen Our Partnerships with the Community by Implementing 'Policing New York in the 1990s.'"[34] And what were the components of the down-graded priority? They were generalized statements without timetables and tasks. Implementation was still waiting for an engineer to get on board.

In retrospect, then, the NYPD did not have a fighting chance for fundamental change. Like many ambitious plans, community policing was foiled by the resistance of the NYPD infrastructure. The "Great Play of Community Policing," as it had proudly billed itself at the outset, had, by its final act, been plagued with poor performances. The negative reviews, some internal, were not surprising. In November 1992, almost two years after community policing's introduction, Commissioner Raymond Kelly installed a small Community Policing Assessment Unit headed by Assistant Chief Aaron Rosenthal. Between November 1992 and August 1993, Rosenthal provided Kelly with twenty-four targeted reports that pulled no punches.[35]

For those pursuing fundamental change, the findings were disheartening. Precinct unit training, as of January 1993, had been a "dismal failure, due to an overall blasé attitude on the part of management, which has filtered down to the attendees." Precinct-level in-service training was "frequently conducted in a haphazard and perfunctory manner" with poor attendance and poorly maintained training logs. In one precinct, the sergeant's presentation "was ill prepared and disjointed." In another precinct, "the training was nonexistent." During one precinct's training session, the training officer implied that foot patrol was burdensome, which was contrary to community-policing philosophy. He referred to the care of radio motor cars with the warning, "We have twenty RMPs [radio motor patrol cars], and one is out of service. If you take care of them, you'll do less foot patrol."[36]

In the field, CPOs were not sharing information about problems such as drug-infested vacant lots with other units and city agencies. Detectives were not informed about precinct crime conditions and did not exchange information with CPOs regarding community activities and needs. Contrary to official policy, auxiliary police officers were not working with CPOs by going on patrol together or sharing information. Community policing officers only rarely assigned themselves to weekend tours, when problems such as prostitution were most frequent.[37] In time, CPOP schedules became less flexible, and turnover accelerated as officers found few incentives to remain in the unit. On the surface, not much had changed; organizational learning was still lacking.

The Legacy of Community Policing

The reformers of the community-policing era could share some ideals and frustrations with reformers from earlier periods. First, they emulated the goals of public involvement, command accountability, and decentralization. Second, they discovered that fundamental change, hampered by inadequate planning and implementation, was extremely difficult. Third, important strides that they made provided the basis for future, rather than immediate, payoffs.

Despite the program's critics, community policing had genuine appeal for some audiences. For many, just the promise of more police generated favorable responses. Those concerned about crime, regardless of neighborhood or class, typically seek additional patrol officers. The notion of returning to the image of the friendly corner cop was inviting, and police officials took advantage of this nostalgia. Beginning in October 1991, the NYPD used posters, radio spots, and vans aggressively to market the slogan "The Beat Cop Is Back."[38]

By and large, a visible and available beat cop was well received by community activists. At the end of 1993, the City Council's Committee on Public Safety held hearings on the NYPD's community-policing program; community board leaders from all five boroughs strongly supported their CPOs. In the words of one Manhattan community leader, the CPO "established a relationship with residents and business residents who desire an officer responsible for a specific area. . . . [P]eople want to see a uniformed presence on the street."[39] A Queens leader observed "an increased degree of familiarity in the general relationship between the community and the police."[40] In the Oceanhill-Brownsville section of Brooklyn, an area long plagued with troubled police–community relations, the local government's district manager gave the new program a ringing endorsement: "[O]ur community has seen a steadfast change in the relationship between the police and the community. . . . [T]here is a visibility of uniformed officers on foot patrol on a daily basis. . . . [T]hese police officers are known by name to the residents and commercial establishments on their beat."[41]

The same community leaders, however, also decried the officers' insufficient numbers, large beat areas, rapid turnover, occasional incivilities, and unpredictable withdrawal from their areas when special events or disturbances arose elsewhere. Though appealing, "the community policing show" exhibited signs of a short run and inadequate backstage support. In the eyes of community leaders, the NYPD did not utilize community-policing techniques as much as other policing activities. It had not fundamentally altered NYPD directions and operations. Contrary to public announcements and "good press," community policing had not become the department's dominant philosophy. Still, it had tapped a market. The community-policing audience was out there. Future police leaders would relearn that lesson.

The CPO's expanded assignment also endowed New York policing in an unexpected way. No longer relying primarily on law enforcement techniques, the beat officer applied the skills of a multitalented problem solver. In a February 1992 department publication, Commissioner Brown raised and answered several questions. His answer to "Aren't We Doing All Those Things Now?" was instructive. "You have been doing an excellent job of pursuing and arresting offenders and answering calls for service as rapidly and efficiently as possible . . . [but] we have not had a strategy for resolving the problems that cause many 911 calls to come from the same locations. . . . [W]e were not organized to reduce and eliminate the conditions that cause crime and fear of crime."[42]

Although the NYPD's problem-solving training was tardy and inadequate, the terms *fear reduction* and *problem-solving officer* became permanent additions to the police lexicon. The technique of diagnosing, analyzing, and tackling crime and quality-of-life incidents for their commonalities and patterns would later become a staple of future, regularized police meetings known as Compstat.

But reducing fear and solving problems were not the only legacies of community policing. Potentially significant changes, little noted at the time, unfolded in an unpredictable fashion. Perhaps this is most evident in the NYPD's adoption and inclusion of legal remedies in its problem-solving approach. This occurred after Commissioner Brown requested that each department unit contribute in some way to community policing's problem solving. The NYPD Legal Bureau responded with a pilot program called the Civil Enforcement Initiative, constituted as the Civil Enforcement Unit (CEU).

Working closely with the precinct commanders, CEU attorneys identified recurring crime and disorder issues and then tailored criminal and civil remedies for each problem. Community trouble spots such as indoor drug markets and prostitution locations were closed for up to a year through nuisance-abatement legal proceedings. These closures clearly diminished illegal activity and deprived landlords of rental income. The padlock and nuisance-abatement laws (described in detail in Chapter 6) closed gambling locations. Street prostitution was addressed through Operation Losing Proposition, whereby female undercover officers posed as street-walking prostitutes and engaged prospective patrons in a conversation that resulted in the arrest of the patron, or "john." Civil enforcement attorneys accompanied the police to evaluate the legal basis for the forfeiture of the would-be customer's vehicle, resulting in arrests and the seizure of automobiles.

The Civil Enforcement Initiative evolved to confront ongoing community problems creatively. For example, Operation Soundtrap addressed the problem of loud car radios utilizing a provision of the Vehicle and Traffic Law (VTL) that makes the loud playing of a car sound system a violation. In cooperation with the Department of Environmental Protection, whose inspectors measured car radio sound levels to determine whether their noise level exceeded the legal limit, the NYPD issued summonses to vehicle operators for violation of the VTL and seized vehicles as evidence.

In June 1991, the Civil Enforcement Unit worked first with the 52nd Precinct in the Bronx, before expanding to three more Bronx precincts in August 1991, and to a Manhattan precinct in July 1992. In a bid to institutionalize civil enforcement and co-ordinate resources at a cross-precinct level, the initiative was expanded in August 1993 (under Commissioner Kelly) to a Queens divisional level that included five precincts. This expansion process would escalate in the post-1993 period.

Conclusion

For the NYPD, 1984–1994 was a turbulent decade. Community and minority protests, first evident in the 1960s, culminated in the expression of pent-up demands for more responsive police services and the expansion of police responsibilities during a period typified by increased fear of crime. Headline events connected with corruption and misconduct stoked numerous external and internal reviews. Reform panels increasingly linked the department's organization and management to police street behavior.

Nowhere was that connection more carefully scrutinized than in the twin reform areas of corruption (which recurred with a ringing frequency) and community policing. Developments in one domain affected the other, and both were stymied by the NYPD's fragmentation, top-down management, inadequate planning, and elusive supervisory processes. The NYPD excelled at shaping its own reaction to external and internal demands for reform, meeting these pressures with predictable stages of organizational resistance. Bureaucratic responses to a corruption crisis were, unfortunately, better geared to quieting that day's demands for reform than to dealing with future corruption problems.

More thought went into announcements about innovations than into their introduction and implementation. Fundamental change, demanding at best, is difficult to advance when there is nothing to sustain it. Inaction reigns when monitoring mechanisms are missing. In a little-known passage in the NYPD's well-publicized community-policing blueprint, Commissioner Brown lauded the recommendations drawn from meetings of his top-flight personnel, which *"provided an opportunity for probing the assumptions that guide the way we do police work. The New York City Police Department is so large that we do not have the opportunity to interact with each other on a regular basis, so the working group's sessions also turned into an important forum for sharing information."* [43] The difficulty of sharing information has consistently plagued the complex, multi-layered NYPD. Compstat's arrival in 1994 represents the most important crack in the NYPD bedrock.

Historically, NYPD's reform efforts, although frequently thwarted, yielded favorable gains. As reform's waves repeatedly struck departmental shores, they left promising residues. New approaches to reducing corruption diminished its intensity and changed its contours, even if these methods did not address all the core issues. Community policing, problem solving, and civil enforcement garnered payoffs and public appeal. These approaches were culled, revised, and stirred in a new post-1993 mix.

4 NEW FACES OF 1994

A 911 call dispatches police officers to a Harlem mosque. They enter, and a melee ensues between the officers and Black Muslims. Afterwards, accusations and recriminations are publicly traded. A representative for the Nation of Islam charges the police with racially motivated brutality, "attacking women and children members in the mosque."[1] The police commissioner dismisses the charges as "outrageous."[2] What really happened, he contends, was that the "cops were overpowered, one of their guns and their radio were taken, and they were literally thrown into the street."[3]

Is this the scene of the April 1972 Harlem Mosque murder (see Chapter 2)? No, this very similar incident, also the result of a hoax, occurred more than two decades later, in January 1994. On the surface, the NYPD's public handling of these episodes was strikingly different, yet the private resolutions of these incidents were not. The duality typifies two faces of the police—official responses to public events and private accords made behind the scenes to "turn down the heat."

The Event: The 1994 Mosque Incident

At 3:57 P.M. on Sunday, January 9, 1994, an anonymous caller reports to the police that an armed robbery is in progress and identifies Muhammad's Mosque No. 7, at Fifth Avenue and 125th Street, as the crime site. "He's sticking up the Muhammad's mosque," the caller says. "He's also selling crack." The voice adds that the gunman has an accomplice who "has a gun, too."[4]

Stories differ as to whether the police at the scene are aware that the building is a mosque. The dispatcher's "signal 30" (robbery in progress) call mentions only the address; therefore, the "sensitive location" policy requiring commanders to be present does not become operational. "They robbed the place at gunpoint," the dispatcher begins. A voice answers, "That's our sector. We'll take it. Have 'em back up."[5] Officers Wendy Jarvis and Paul Palombo, both on the force for only a year and a half, are the first to respond. There is no sign identifying the nondescript building as a mosque; it houses a supermarket on the first level, the mosque and a gym on the third floor.

Later, Police Commissioner William Bratton contended, "A report of a firearm is very serious, and the officers had every right—indeed, the duty—to investigate thoroughly."[6] Spokesmen for the Nation of Islam did not buy that argument. The Reverend Al Sharpton insisted, "I think if it was another religious institution in another community, [the police] coming in during a service would not have been tolerated."[7]

The Public Face

The January 9 incident occurred at a critical time, eight days after Rudolph Giuliani's installation as the city's 107th mayor and one day before Bratton officially took over as NYPD's 38th police commissioner. Although there were no fatalities, the mosque event resurfaced in the public's mind two days later when the seventeen-year-old black son of a famous Muslim cleric was fatally shot by a white police officer. The public statements and executive actions of the mayor and commissioner were closely scrutinized for indications of the new administration's policies on crime and law enforcement. What signals were being given to the street cops and to the public, including the minority community, which had given Giuliani only 5 percent of its votes?

Law enforcement flares were quickly lit by the new mayor and police commissioner. Giuliani and Bratton were in frequent phone contact during the incident, and their public statements were in sync during the ensuing days. Bratton, referring to the confrontation as "sheer terror" for the police, complained that "leaders of the Harlem mosque reneged on a promise to surrender a suspect in the attacks on the officers."[8] Bratton characterized his and the mayor's common approach: "The mayor believed that where there is room for the benefit of the doubt, the benefit should go to the police. . . . Our early comments to the press said just that."[9]

Giuliani insisted that the assault on the officers was the main issue and that it was "unacceptable conduct." His response to questions about his willingness to meet with black leaders was positive but qualified: "If they have an open mind, that would be terrific. If they want to create a media event and a distortion of what occurred, that doesn't help the city."[10]

The mayor and commissioner wanted to present to the public a new face: reverence for law and order. The mosque incident provided a golden opportunity—a "gift," the commissioner called it[11]—to broadcast this message. Nowhere was this contrast with the past more visible than in the commissioner's post-mosque meeting with Muslim leaders.

The 1972 meeting with Black Muslim leaders had been marked by Mayor Lindsay and Commissioner Murphy's reluctance to issue "information that conceivably could provoke a reaction and possibly violence. Silence was the thing." Their public statements struck the police rank and file as inadequate. Lindsay's and Murphy's failure to condemn the Muslims for the death of an officer may have sent a message of restraint to the public, but it produced a shock wave within the NYPD that eroded confidence in the top brass. Commissioner Murphy blamed poor NYPD management for the failure to honor the "sensitive locations" agreement when the officers entered the mosque. Thus, when Murphy met with Minister Louis Farrakhan, the Muslim leader, NYPD's position was already compromised. "He [Farrakhan] didn't have to be brilliant," Murphy recalled, "to know that he had us over the barrel. That was what made me uncomfortable, what had made it impossible to deny the minister's request for an interview." [12]

In contrast with the 1972 meeting, the 1994 meeting followed sterner police statements, and as a result, it was immediately embroiled in controversy. On January 13, four days after the incident, Minister Don Muhammad, whom Bratton already knew, and Minister Conrad Muhammad from the 125th Street mosque arrived at headquarters for a scheduled meeting with the commissioner. To the surprise of the commissioner, C. Vernon Mason, an attorney, and Reverend Al Sharpton, a local activist, also appeared. Bratton, declining to meet with all of them, canceled the meeting. He remarked, "It was inappropriate to have that meeting with a larger than intended group and get into areas [including legal issues] I was not prepared to discuss." [13] Mason and Sharpton both were *personae non grata* with the police. They were controversial figures who ignited strong emotions and were anathema to much of the public. Bratton believed that Sharpton's recent "rabble rousing around a black boycott of a Korean grocery store was shamefully destructive to the city's race relations and had undermined the administration of Mayor Dinkins and his police commissioner, Lee Brown." [14] Mayor Giuliani observed, "We have spent way too much time on Reverend Sharpton than it's really worth." Sharpton accused Giuliani and Bratton of "playing a divide-and-conquer strategy by accepting some leaders and denying others." [15]

The Private Face

Meanwhile, as the public and cops on the street looked on attentively, backstage bartering was taking place. The commissioner and Muslim leaders met "secretly"[16] at a Wall Street brokerage firm the day after the canceled meeting. There was no press coverage.[17] The Muslims contended that the police disrespectfully rushed into the mosque, and would have avoided this kind of display at a church or synagogue. In Bratton's view, "The point had some legitimacy; the officers could have shown more sensitivity, and perhaps if they had entered a religious location they were more familiar with, they would have." Participants at this meeting, according to the commissioner, "agreed, in good faith, to disagree. The Muslims refused to turn over any suspects, and the police department told them we didn't need any help; we would catch the criminals on our own."[18] This private agreement differed little from the widely criticized (especially by the rank-and-file police) resolution of the 1972 conflict.

Nor was this the only parallel. Although the 1994 episode was less violent than the 1972 event, police and Muslims were at a standoff during both incidents. During the 1994 episode, after officers Jarvis and Palombo were overwhelmed by insiders at the mosque and tossed out onto the icy winter street, a crowd gathered. Backup police were called, and the Muslims, refusing them entry, claimed the police were holding them hostage in the building.

As in the earlier event, police on the scene in 1994 negotiated with the Muslims. Chief Joseph Leake, Manhattan's borough commander, was in charge of the discussions, and he faced powerful, conflicting pressures. On the one hand, Mayor Giuliani, in constant radio contact with Leake, urged an assault on the mosque to arrest those who attacked the police and to recover the department's gun and radio. On the other hand, Leake had established strong ties with the community. One mosque minister with whom he had a good relationship confided that it "was not wise to go in and make arrests because there would be many other Muslims from all over coming there to raise a disturbance." Leake responded that he "could not allow them [the suspects] to go without an arrest." There was a compromise: the police could search the mosque for the missing gun and radio (which they found). The Muslims could leave the mosque, but must file out singly so that those who took part in the assault could be identified. The Muslims promised to produce the perpetrators the next day, and the mayor reluctantly signed off on the agreement.

As in 1972, the Muslims did not uphold their promise to produce the perpetrators. But, as noted, Commissioner Bratton dropped this point at the closed meeting with Muslim leaders five days after the incident. Bratton was sensitive to community concerns, and in private he faced the political reality of the situation—the Muslims were important parts of a minority constituency. The 1972 street disturbances outside the mosque could not be repeated. To enter the mosque, Bratton believed, "would exacerbate the situation." Besides, Bratton felt, the department had made a "serious mistake"[19] when the police entered without knowing that this was a "sensitive location." Twenty-two years earlier, Commissioner Murphy had also understood the volatility of police entrance into a mosque.

Despite the glaring differences in public behavior, therefore, the NYPD's 1972 and 1994 private faces were virtual look-alikes. But astute leaders know that a strong public image is vital to the police role and can contribute to the beat cop's morale. As one officer put it, "There was a new sheriff in town." The police would not be swayed by minority communities. Violations of the law, particularly attacks on police, would be pursued regardless of the consequences. Given the motif of law and order in candidate Giuliani's mayoral bid, his position on the mosque incident was not surprising. The 1993 campaign accurately foreshadowed law enforcement's new public face.

Campaign Critique

It is surprising, at first glance, that Giuliani was so successful in using law enforcement issues in his election campaign. Under incumbent Mayor David Dinkins's $1.8 billion Safe Streets–Safe Cities program, the NYPD's authorized strength had been increased, so that as the election campaign heated up, 3,500 of the authorized 6,000 patrol officers were already on the streets. All seventy-five precincts had community police officers, who generally were well received. Community leaders also welcomed the precinct management teams, which met regularly to deal with neighborhood problems, and included police supervisors, community board district managers, members of the precinct community councils, and other residents. Furthermore, crime rates were declining during the Dinkins administration. This downward trend began with a 1990 decrease of .03 percent from the preceding year. In 1991 crime declined 4.4 percent from the 1990 rate, and in 1992 it dropped another 7.8 percent. Voters presumably would have had every reason to be pleased with Dinkins's crime control policies.

Countering other explanations for the decrease, such as a decline in crack use and trade, Dinkins credited his administration with better crime fighting. The crime statistics, however, did not alleviate the prevailing public fear of crime. Many citizens regarded the Dinkins administration as unable or unwilling to restrain random and impulsive criminal acts. Two controversial events that occurred early in the mayor's administration fueled this perception and kept incumbent Dinkins perched on law enforcement's defensive ledge.

The Korean Grocer Boycott.   The initial incident occurred in January 1990, shortly after Dinkins was sworn into office, and simmered publicly for more than a year. Gieslaine Felissaint, a forty-seven-year-old home care worker born in Haiti, alleged that she had been accused of shoplifting, slapped three times in the face by a Korean grocer, and then punched, kicked, and knocked to the floor by two store employees. These injuries, Ms. Felissaint claimed, kept her out of work for months. Pong Ok Jang, owner and manager of the Family Red Apple grocery store in Flatbush, Brooklyn, contended that Felissaint caused a commotion by throwing pepper in the cashier's face. He tried to calm her and usher her out of the store, but she sat down on the floor and screamed.

This episode ignited a black-led boycott of Mr. Pong's grocery and of a Korean fruit market directly across the street, which had allegedly sheltered a Family Red Apple employee after the confrontation with Ms. Felissaint. Reverend Al Sharpton and Sonny Carson, another controversial community activist, were key figures in the boycott demonstrations. Protesters picketed against the treatment of Ms. Felissaint and the dominance of successful Korean businesses in poor black neighborhoods. They distributed a pamphlet that read in part: "The real question for black folks to consider in the 1990s is who is going to control the economic life of the black community?"[20]

Mayor Dinkins was reluctant to inflame passions by taking sides, and he sought to end the boycott by mediation, an approach he had used successfully to resolve a similar boycott. Five months into the Red Apple boycott, Justice Gerald Held granted the Korean families an injunction prohibiting gatherings outside their businesses and requiring protesters to remain at least fifty feet from the stores' entrances. Judge Held was critical of the mayor's "failure . . . to personally intervene and use the prestige of his office and his standing in the community to convince the parties to bring a suitable end to this dispute."[21]

The NYPD declined to enforce the injunction on the basis of a City Corporation Counsel ruling that the police were not party to the lawsuit. The department also contended that its discretionary power allowed it to select negotiation rather than confrontation to resolve such disputes.

The mayor continued to be criticized for not doing enough to settle the boycott. Laura Blackburne, cochair of the mayoral committee on the Korean grocery boycott, appeared before the City Council in September. Assemblyman Mel Miller, representing Flatbush, assailed Blackburne and Dinkins at that meeting, demanding that she and the mayor shop at the boycotted Korean store as a "symbolic statement against the protest."[22]

Also in September, an appellate court upheld the injunction to keep protesters away from the Korean store entrances and sharply rejected the NYPD's legal claims, in which the department had absolved itself of enforcement duties. The unanimous decision of the four-judge panel declared, "The police department is sworn to uphold enforcement of the city charter," and noted, "It shall be the [department's] duty to disperse unlawful or dangerous assemblages which obstruct the free passage of public streets [and] sidewalks . . . and prevent the violation of all laws and ordinances." Furthermore, the court pointedly added, the NYPD cannot decide for itself the most effective enforcement of a court order.

The court's commentary stung more than its ruling. "The boycott," the court found, was often "volatile and racially charged in tone, resulting in several instances of violence, as the demonstrators, using bullhorns and positioning themselves in close proximity to the store entrances, exhorted and, in certain instances, verbally abused shoppers, in order to dissuade them from patronizing the petitioners' establishments." The court found that potential "community resentment or community hostility" could not be used by the Dinkins administration or the NYPD as a basis for declining to enforce the court order.[23]

The police department abided by this order, keeping protesters fifty feet from the stores' entrances, but the boycott continued. In January 1991, a year after the initial incident, a jury acquitted Mr. Pong, the manager of the Korean grocery, of an assault charge. Asked if the verdict would end the boycott and return his customers, Mr. Pong said, "I don't know. I was not guilty, and outside there are protesters."[24] The number of participants decreased, but the lingering boycott, left unresolved and festering, fueled condemnation of the mayor.

The perception that the Dinkins administration practiced uneven law enforcement was hammered home by Giuliani during the election campaign. Even before the campaign officially began, Giuliani was on the offensive, attacking Dinkins in the *New York Times* for "failing to control street agitators boycotting a Korean grocer in Brooklyn, despite a court order to do so."[25] During the campaign, Giuliani declared, "I would have enforced the court order that said the boycotters should be kept 50 feet away. And I would have enforced it the first moment I found out about it, not six months later."[26]

Subsequent events often were viewed through the prism of the Korean boycott. But no event aroused more controversy and misgivings about the Dinkins administration's commitment to law enforcement than the 1991 Crown Heights incident.

Crown Heights.   The Crown Heights drama not only claimed the attention of much of the city's Jewish community, but also emerged as a defining law enforcement event with broad repercussions for the Dinkins administration. Violence arose on August 19, 1991, after a seven-year-old black child, Gavin Cato, was fatally struck by a car in a Lubavitcher orthodox Jewish motorcade in Crown Heights, a religiously and ethnically diverse Brooklyn community. The driver was a member of the Lubavitcher sect. A false rumor—that an ambulance operated by a private Jewish organization failed to help the child—heightened the chaos. Yankel Rosenbaum, a visiting twenty-nine-year-old Australian who was a Hasidic scholar, was fatally stabbed during the first several hours of the rioting. Black youths marauded through the neighborhood; demonstrators firebombed stores and cars; and militants hurled rocks and concrete at journalists and police officials, and even threw bottles at Mayor Dinkins when he left the Cato family apartment. Eight police officers were hospitalized after being hit by buckshot fired from a roof. It took several days to restore order.

The issues of unruly violence and inadequate police response were intertwined with those of race and religion. Mayoral accountability became the focus of accusations. Had Dinkins hamstrung police crowd control, thereby enabling violence to escalate? The police publicly acknowledged tactical errors and the lack of a coherent crowd-control deployment strategy.

In October 1992, the accused murderer of Yankel Rosenbaum, seventeen-year-old Lemrick Nelson, Jr., was acquitted, contrary to expectations. Rosenbaum's brother, Norman, stood outside the courthouse and protested, "Lemrick Nelson is a murderer. . . . He is a guilty person unfairly acquitted." This verdict put Crown Heights back on the front page and stoked demonstrations and accusations of inadequate and biased police work. Within a month, the Lubavitcher group initiated a federal lawsuit against Nelson and accused the mayor and the former police commissioner Lee Brown of "withholding police protective services on a discriminatory and selective basis," thereby violating Yankel Rosenbaum's civil rights. The suit charged the police with negligence, having permitted blacks "to vent their rage" after the death of Gavin Cato "at the expense of the lives and property of Jews and other non-blacks present in the Crown Heights community."[27]

Crown Heights passions persisted, and the mayor's standing declined. Dinkins pleaded with citizens not to make Crown Heights a "litmus test" for elected officials. Late in the fall of

1992, he delivered a major television address to "defuse the anger." Speaking forcefully about the deaths in Crown Heights and referring to the police response, Dinkins accepted personal responsibility and promised to prevent future NYPD "tactical errors in judgment and deployment of police officers." Months later, in front of City Hall, the mayor stood surrounded by much of the city's Jewish establishment. "I've made mistakes," he said. "I recognize that, but I've learned from my mistakes, and I won't make those mistakes again."[28]

The political firestorm spread during the summer of 1993, which was a time of passionate political campaigning. After much speculation in the press as to its contents, a special state commission's report on the Crown Heights racial violence was issued. The report identified a "leadership vacuum at the highest levels" of city government during "the most extensive racial unrest in New York City in 20 years." The city, the report continued, allowed the rioting to continue for days before ordering more aggressive policing. Police Commissioner [Brown] "failed to fulfill his ultimate responsibility" during the episode.[29]

Clearly on the defensive, the mayor again acknowledged his "personal responsibility" for the safety of New York's citizens, and he pledged, "Never again will any group in our city feel it did not receive the police protection that it has the right to expect." The new police commissioner, Ray Kelly, commented: "What the report says is that the Police Department did not respond quickly enough. . . . We accept that point."[30] But Governor Mario Cuomo went a step further, saying it was more than slow mobilization of the police; the Crown Heights riot "was handled badly."[31]

Dinkins's castle door was now assailable by candidate Giuliani's battering ram. Giuliani said, "I believe if I were Mayor of New York City, they would have made arrests the first moment that a rock was thrown through a store window, a car was burned or a person was beaten up because they were Jewish, or for any

other reason. And I certainly . . . would have investigated it my-
self and not waited 22 months."[32]

The Korean boycott and Crown Heights violence became
staging areas for Giuliani's law enforcement campaign, virtually
obliterating Dinkins's public safety achievements. Giuliani used
hard-hitting and effective rhetoric ("If he can't manage a riot, he
can't manage a boycott . . .") and television and radio spots that
highlighted law enforcement as his campaign's centerpiece. He
used every opportunity to assail the "disorder that is driving the
city down." Dinkins was charged with failure to address petty
street crime, narcotics dealing, and other aspects of quality of
life in the city. Giuliani depicted some streets and communities,
such as Washington Heights, as "overwhelmed by drug deals,"
with criminals roaming "unhindered by arrest." He promised
to increase drug arrests and to harvest guns from the street. He
would arrest panhandlers and "squeegee men" if they used in-
timidation and threats of bodily harm that could be legally clas-
sified as assault. Giuliani backers supported their candidate because he promised to address what they declared to be unchecked
crime, and they pointed to the violence in Crown Heights and
Flatbush as examples. Despite tumbling crime statistics under
Dinkins's administration, 59 percent of voters polled a month
before the election declared the city less safe than four years earlier, and 46 percent said that crime remained a major issue.[33]

Crime Motifs. Crime events and the political firestorm of a
tight mayoral race encouraged Giuliani to focus on law enforcement. Despite the rhetoric, however, it was clear after the election that the central components of the new administration's
crime fighting, while significant, proved to be neither novel nor
untested. Their contours had been foreshadowed by previous police operations.

It was hard to argue that averting crime, even nuisance crime
or incivility, before it erupts is better than reacting to ongoing,

more violent criminal activity. Low-level drug dealing, aggressive panhandling, illegal street peddling, noise, prostitution, graffiti, loitering, public urination, pickpocketing, disorderly premises, and illegal social clubs all cried out for attention. Giuliani
knew that these nuisances heightened fear and detracted from
the public's sense of well-being and of entitlement to a good
"quality of life"; he also knew that "threshold crime" breeds
disorder, a community's decline, and, eventually, more serious
crime.

Giuliani was following an honorable tradition. The NYPD's
first patrol guide addressed crime prevention (see Chapter 2).
Post-1970s reformers promoted community policing's ability to
reduce all crime, and Commissioner Lee Brown later sought to
upgrade the department's capacity "to reduce and eliminate the
conditions that cause crime and fear of crime."[34]

The connection between neighborhood orderliness, fear reduction, and crime was persuasively advanced in an acclaimed 1982
article by James Q. Wilson and George Kelling, who championed
police strategies to prevent low-level social disorders, such as
broken windows and graffiti, from spiraling out of control. Urban dwellers most frequently complained about daily indigni-
ties—street noise, neighborhood prostitution, and other signs of
decay, which were believed to embolden criminals to ply their
trade.[35]

The argument for preventive crime fighting resonated with
the policies of Mayor Giuliani and his police commissioner.
Many street cops had long made a connection between low-level
disorder and predatory crime. They knew that public drunken-
ness, gambling, and prostitution often escalate into fights, robberies, and shootings. In 1980, the Fund for the City of New York
undertook a little-known study of police patrol and street conditions in the Times Square area. Their report, prepared a year before Wilson and Kelling's "broken windows" article, refers to a
1978 analysis of Times Square:

Police and other enforcement officials believe that certain types of street conditions such as the number, type, and frequency of street solicitations, the number of individuals loitering in doorways, and storefront uses and their hours of operations do contribute to, or have the potential to contribute to, serious crime. At the very least, offensive street conditions are perceived as dangerous and threatening to the public and are a major reason for avoidance of an area, especially in the evening hours. They are a primary contributor to the negative image of Times Square held by most New York area residents and tourists, and are part of a self-perpetuating cycle of decay, well documented in the City University of New York's West 42nd Street study.[36]

As New York Transit police chief from 1990 to 1992, Bratton had pushed for full enforcement of all subway rules and regulations with a targeted attack on fare beating and disorderly conduct. Fare evasions dropped, and the police discovered that many of those arrested had outstanding warrants for robberies and other serious crimes. Commissioner Ray Kelly, Bratton's predecessor, had applied quality-of-life enforcement in a successful 1993 campaign to curb unsolicited car window washing, known as squeegeeing. The squeegee men menacingly and sometimes violently approached cars that were backed up at entrances and exits to highways, bridges, and tunnels. About half of the squeegee men arrested had previous arrests for serious felonies, and a majority had previous drug-related offenses. Commissioners Bratton and Kelly extended the option of using civil enforcement laws to address quality-of-life offenses such as deafening radio boom boxes and invasive street prostitution.

Orchestrating Change

Postulating anticrime measures is one thing; making them work is another. The mayor and new commissioner followed precedent: Command accountability and decentralized police bureaucracy were again advanced as the route to the land of reform. An assemblage of field soldiers and officers, as in the first act of *Aida*, would deliver on the top command's promise to dramatically reduce crime. But the stumbling of previous reform administrations on a stage replete with bureaucratic land mines and social "snafus" had shown the need for more deftness and sophistication in reconfiguring the NYPD bureaucracy. New orchestration—familiar refrains sprinkled with new tunes—was key to renovation under the firm hands of the mayor and commissioner, the producer and director. This approach by the new administration was critical to the NYPD's successful performance on such a grand scale.

Reengineering.   Modern management provided the orchestral score; "reengineering" was its name. Contemporary management literature explained that reengineering requires "radical change," a "starting over" throughout the entire organization, nothing less than a "reinvention of how organizations work."[37] Commissioner Bratton insisted: "We reengineered the NYPD into an organization capable of supporting our goals."[38] The commissioner contended that he "involved more than three hundred people from every NYPD rank and bureau" in twelve reengineering teams.[39] Reporters were captivated by the reengineering motif and the "Management Secrets of Crime-Fighter Extraordinaire William Bratton."[40] The *New Yorker* described "The CEO Cop" as "an avid consumer of the literature of corporate reorganization and motivation."[41] The commissioner was portrayed by the *Economist* as "a fan of the re-engineering rhetoric of Michael Hammer and James Champy."[42] *Business Week* lauded the NYPD's "innovative turnaround artists" who used "private-sector" techniques.[43]

These public statements, however, were longer on praise than on analysis. In private interviews and in print, Bratton repeatedly contended that his teams "surveyed nearly eight thousand cops and eventually made more than six hundred recommendations, of which 80 percent were eventually accepted."[44] No documentation of this oft-repeated claim was offered; yet it was echoed by such prestigious institutions as the Harvard Business School. Its case study of the Bratton reorganization reported, "The [reengineering] process produced more than 600 recommendations, 80 percent of which were implemented."[45] An internal NYPD reengineering "Implementation Report," however, flatly states that the "twelve committees submitted a collective total of 418 recommendations." In reality, this number was reduced further when the commissioner appointed "a plan of action committee" to "use the recommendations of the reengineering teams as a base in developing a preliminary plan of action. In doing so, over two hundred of the remaining recommendations were touched upon with many being expanded or modified."[46] Bratton's 600-plus recommendations had thus been cut by two-thirds, yielding, at the 80 percent adoption rate, 160 implemented changes. Nor is there any backing for even this modified calculation.

In actuality, the top brass did the whittling. The plan of action committee included no patrol officers, sergeants, or lieutenants. The fifteen members ranged from deputy inspector to chief, with only two captains. This committee was as exclusive as the twelve reengineering committees, all of which were heavily weighted with top brass. One lesser-ranking committee member of a reengineering committee recalls his participation: "I was called on a Monday for a Tuesday meeting. They needed one of us. I showed up." The reengineering teams, then, supplied a communal endorsement for new top-level directives. As one high-ranking official put it, "There were no surprises in reengineering. It delivered what we expected. We could now go to the troops and say, 'You told us what the problems are and we listened.'"

Harmonizing the Score. Reengineering was less discovery and more recovery. The committees were stacked with change advocates seeking to reclaim the past. In a climate ripe for assailing prevailing policies as woefully inadequate, reengineering was the wedge used by Bratton and his supporters to restructure the NYPD. Each of twelve reengineering teams was dedicated to a specific topic[47] and was asked to determine what was broken and how to fix it—or, perhaps more accurately, what would be used to replace it. Each committee was supplied with a copy of Hammer and Champy's *Reengineering the Corporation,* which advocated "abandoning outdated rules and fundamental assumptions."[48]

The reengineering reports questioned the NYPD's operating procedures. The results of the current policy, they claimed, was inadequate. The precinct organization report noted:

> 2 or 3 percent reduction in crime is not good enough. We need
> to change the organization to do more. The need to reengineer
> precincts is not immediately apparent. City-wide crime continues
> to decline year after year. Every annual precinct state of com-
> mand report, without exception, includes evidence of neighbor-
> hood improvements. Bureau and Special Unit Commanders to
> a man, or a woman, will vigorously defend the effectiveness
> of the present system. Why fix what's not broken?
>
> The answer is in the new mission of the department to dra-
> matically reduce crime, fear, and disorder. Slow, continuous im-
> provement doesn't cut it, and that is all the present system can
> deliver. . . . [R]e-engineering in its simplest forms means starting
> all over, starting from scratch.[49]

Reengineering acted like a booster cable to the NYPD's battery, providing the cranking power needed to activate decentralization and command accountability. Relinquishing control of daily ground operations was the most fundamental yet difficult challenge facing the new administration. Traditionally, the person at the apex of the NYPD pyramid would retain control through standardized procedures and policies. But in order to hold precinct commanders accountable for crime prevention, the new leadership knew the organization must grant them more discretion. Rather than allow headquarters to determine staffing and deployment on a citywide basis, it was decided that reducing crime, fear of crime, and disorder would flow from patrol borough and precinct coordination of selected enforcement efforts.

The reengineering reports sought to "empower" precinct commanders to customize and implement their own crime-fighting plans, thereby shifting the NYPD from a routine of patrol-and-arrest activities to one weighted toward results. Commanding officers (COs) were authorized to allow their anticrime units to perform decoy operations, a function that had previously been left to the Citywide Street Crime Unit. Precinct personnel were permitted to execute felony arrests warrants, and COs could use plainclothes officers for vice enforcement activities. Patrol cops were encouraged to make drug arrests and to enforce quality-of-life laws. Headquarters' restrictions on the total number of personnel that precinct commanders could assign to their own "specialty units" (for instance, street narcotics units) were lifted. These operational moves were significant departures from the NYPD's long-standing practice of prohibiting precinct personnel from conducting sensitive, corruption-prone enforcement activities.

The New Players.   Without the participation of new change advocates as replacements for the old guard, reengineering would have been little more than a catchy managerial fad. Before he had left Boston to assume his new position, Bratton announced his intention to "reshuffle the ranking commanders at One Police Plaza [police headquarters]." Within the first month, significant personnel changes were made.

The process was instructive. The day before he took office, Bratton requested undated resignations from the department's fifteen highest-ranking officials. Another early order directed top-level bureau chiefs to submit crime reduction plans for their areas of responsibility. It was presumed that a good plan would permit a chief to remain in his job. This order triggered a mad scramble for plans, any plans—some new and some old. However, the commissioner rejected all the proposals. Some observers believed the exercise was a device to expose the old regime, showing that there was more it could have been doing but did not until threatened with retirement. Two weeks later, Bratton dated the resignation letters from four of the highest-ranking officers and announced that he was going to shake off "the drift and passivity and laissez-faire that I sense in the organization."[50]

After Bratton's first month in office, the first deputy commissioner, chief of patrol, chief of the Management Information Bureau, chief of the Organized Crime Control Bureau (OCCB), chief of detectives, chief of personnel, deputy commissioner for community affairs, and others had retired and been replaced by mostly middle-ranking officers with reputations for being aggressive risk takers. These were early and swift personnel replacements by a commissioner who prided himself on rapid and effective change. In addition, Bratton replaced more than two-thirds of the city's seventy-six precinct commanders during the first year of his administration. In contrast, former reform commissioner Murphy's slow and methodical 90 percent replacement of top-level personnel was staggered over a thirty-one-month period.

The incoming command personnel were known by the "foot soldiers" as activists and champions of anticrime initiatives. Bratton created a new position, deputy commissioner for crime control strategies, for his former aide Jack Maple. A colorful investigative lieutenant in the New York Transit Police, Maple had been a special assistant when Bratton headed the NYC Transit Police. Maple's prominent NYPD ranking as deputy commissioner was described as "roughly equivalent to an ensign in the Coast Guard waking up one day as a three-star admiral."[51] The new deputy commissioner sought to steer the NYPD away from its traditional defensive position of damage control, toward a proactive stance based on informed anticrime battle plans. "No general went to war without a map," he said.

NYPD Deputy Chief John F. Timoney, a well-respected field tactician and innovative crime analyst known for his candor, became the top uniformed officer. At age forty-five, Timoney was the youngest chief of the department. He had leaped over senior officers, from those with one star to the highest four-star chief, shaking up the police hierarchy and signaling Bratton's zeal for change. "Too many bosses," Timoney believed, "had kept a low profile. We had to smoke out phonies who claimed the department does not let us do our job while they were using this as a curtain for inaction." Timoney replaced David W. Scott, who had been promoted by Bratton to first deputy commissioner. A well-regarded chief, Scott was one of the few high-ranking commanders of the previous regime to remain with the new administration.

Timoney and Scott linked Bratton to the bureaucratic back bench, the up-and-coming activists, and helped fashion the new leadership lineup. A third key player was Louis R. Anemone, whose career included command of three precincts; he was promoted to chief of patrol, a two-star jump. Anemone viewed the NYPD's recent past as "lost direction with no focus on crime fighting. We were there to keep the lid on and not to be an embarrassment. The main thing was don't make waves, something might go wrong. You were put through the ringer if you really did your job." Anemone was well known by the troops for his activist style. A year later, he was promoted to chief of department, replacing Timoney, who had moved into Scott's position. Scott retired from his new role as first deputy commissioner for health reasons.

Chief Patrick E. Kelleher, another notable figure in the executive lineup, served in the critical position of executive officer in Anemone's chief of patrol office. Kelleher saw a vivid distinction "between the old way and new way of collecting [data] and examining crime." The "old way" was reactive and dated. A year later, Kelleher, known as a savvy, productive workaholic with a diverse police background, was promoted to chief of the Internal Affairs Bureau. Martin O'Boyle, with strong narcotics combat experience, was also recognized in the early selection process. He was promoted to deputy chief and elevated to head the Narcotics Division. O'Boyle believed that NYPD units had been "in their own silos—limited in joint actions" on such overlapping problems as drugs and guns. Bratton viewed him as "a man who's been with the troops. We want bosses with hands-on experience." A year later, O'Boyle was advanced to head the Organized Crime Control Bureau.

Bratton's swift convening of his young team delivered a clear message—promotions would be based on performance and promise, not on length of service. In Timoney's words, "Some people formerly got to the top by sticking around longer than anyone else." The wide-ranging field experiences of the top command enabled the new NYPD leadership team to stay in touch with the troops in the field. As former commissioner Murphy observed in 1977, the "lower 90 percent of a department will take its cues from the top 10 percent." Murphy believed this 10 percent was perceived by the rank and file as divided "into two contending factions—the good guys and the bad guys." The new administrator ought to advance the good guys with whom "the younger, more idealistic, more potentially productive officers" in the lower ranks identify.[52]

Merchandising the Message

The department marketed a message: Crime would be reduced substantially through assertive policing. Entrance to Bratton's higher echelon was restricted to commanders committed to double-digit crime reduction. The establishment of a specific objective—a 10 percent reduction in crime for 1994—was the initial propellant for change. While target setting is the norm for the private sector, it usually is anathema for public organizations because it offers a yardstick against which performance can be more accurately measured and, if deficient, condemned. Some of Bratton's top aides, reflecting traditional bureaucratic caution, advised him against making this public commitment to reduce crime by a quantifiable amount. "I told him he was flirting with media disaster and cynicism," recalls one former top official. The commissioner, however, was aware of the power of goal setting as a focus and a rallying cry for action. Specific goals, as Bratton knew, operate as mobilizers of personnel, enabling an organization to see that old ways do not work and that one must "push the envelope" in order to reach new heights.

Like Patrick Murphy, police commissioner from October 1970 to May 1973, Bratton was a devotee of modern management literature. Bratton saw himself more as a CEO than as a "PC" (as the police commissioner is called inside the department). Bratton, however, had distinct advantages over Murphy. First, he had the initial solid backing of a mayor who wanted him to move rapidly. Second, he knew contemporary management scholarship had shifted its focus from the rigidities of relationships among formal positions to behavioral connections between employees and their work. Current "reengineering" approaches emphasized cultural change and shared values, leadership and communications, risk taking and starting anew, vision and purpose, crisis and opportunity, morale and motivation. These new approaches were vitally important for enlisting a critical mass of the cops in crime-prevention strategies. Third, Bratton benefited from studying Murphy's experience. He understood that rapid personnel changes were preferable to replacement strategies that extended over a long period of time.

Goal setting was a mobilizer and an organizing framework for communicating changes, but it was not sufficient. Bratton's new leaders appreciated that creating shared values requires frequent repetition of ideas. Reinforcing messages have to be sent and received. The commissioner's numerous field visits, on which he was accompanied by his new top-level command, were vivid examples of this reinforcing process. Although brief, there were also conversations with cops on the street. Crime-fighting messages were prominent. In the crime strategy conference "war room," officially known as the Command and Control Center, a sign, prominently posted, read: "We are not just report takers— we are the police." This mind-set contrasted starkly with 1980s police mission and value statements, which more often than not were empty slogans with little street impact. The NYPD's pre-Bratton, community-policing "values" statements began: "In partnership with the community we pledge to protect the lives and property of our fellow citizens and impartially enforce the law." The message usually was ignored and certainly was less punchy than the new slogan.

Motivational messages about crime reduction were also delivered through other channels. The new administration's indefatigable communications machinery churned out departmental-strategy training videos and newsletters. Contacts with news organizations and union delegates were cultivated. Bratton, acutely aware that the troops were part of a public audience that could be reached through the media, publicized incidents such as the tossing of a panhandler off a subway car. In this way, he signaled to the rank and file the importance of quality-of-life issues. In another watershed event, Bratton made good press by publicly confiscating the badges of Harlem precinct officers who were accused in his first corruption scandal. Disgraced badge numbers would no longer be used by future department members. The commissioner's aggressive and dramatic methods for dealing with internal corruption symbolized the new administration's rejection of the NYPD's traditional defensive attitude.

Bratton was a master of the sound bite. An admirer of Churchill, he frequently referred to "taking back the city, street by street, block by block." He widened access to the department for the press, researchers, and others. The press welcomed pre-packaged communications messages. Some carefully cultivated members of the media were offered advance information about personnel changes, upcoming crime strategies, and crime data. Given entry to the inner sanctum, tabloids responded with favorable stories. Thus, Bratton's crime reduction messages were repeated frequently, helping to push the police force into an aggressive law enforcement mind-set.

Cataloging the Message.   Messages are critical. Cops must buy in. But Bratton's messages did not guarantee his ability to change long-standing practices. His new crime strategies had to overcome the NYPD's persistent centralization, fragmentation, top-down management, and elusive supervisory processes. Bratton, believing that the key to change was a sense of crisis, contrasted his arrival in the New York Transit Police with his arrival in the NYPD:

> Organizations can change the most when they are in crises. When I came to the New York Transit Police, it was clear to everyone that the department was in crisis, with crime escalating and morale very low. With the NYPD, we had to create a crisis since there was no crisis of confidence. The prevailing view was that we did things well. We are the best. There is no one any better. So the strategies and reengineering process were intended to create a crisis and a process to move the organization through changes. . . . It was revolutionary.

While the reengineering teams were formulating their proposals, Bratton was publicizing a general call to arms: The city was in the grip of rampant crime with an ineffective police response. Between March and July of 1994, the NYPD issued five documents intended to substitute strategic direction for micromanagement. (See Appendix A for a listing of strategies.) Cobbled together by some of the key reengineering participants, these strategies (on guns, drugs, youth violence, domestic violence, and reclaiming public spaces) deplored criminal conditions and police inaction.

The publicized strategies offered back-to-basics game plans for addressing deplorable and unacceptable conditions. Strategy Number One, "Getting Guns off the Streets of New York," discussed the percentage increase in gun-related homicides and their impact on public fear and medical costs. The document noted, "Whatever we are doing to reduce violent—especially handgun-related crime—is not working." [53] Procedures for gun seizures were criticized for the lack of follow-up investigations and coordination and their failure to halt illegal gun trafficking. The report noted that gun arrests were low in number and that the confiscation rate for felony weapons had dropped dramatically because of inadequate officer training. The new strategy directed officers to pursue gun traffickers aggressively and called for detectives to thoroughly debrief all prisoners. The strategy on gun control advocated improved training and greater cooperation between street patrol and specialized detective units.

The various strategies systematically presented familiar crime-fighting techniques that worked. The second strategy, "Curbing Youth Violence in the Schools and on the Street," refocused patrol and detective efforts on truant hangouts. It also coordinated the use of youth offender databases so that known behavioral patterns could be matched with unsolved crimes. This approach echoed that of a Brooklyn precinct's anticrime unit which in 1982 traced clusters of crime to particular truants. The Brooklyn precinct conducted meetings of all units and returned truants to their schools, cutting the area's daytime robberies in half. Similarly, Bratton's 1994 strategy called for truancy teams "to locate and return to the schools designated by the Chancellor the thousands of truants at large on any school day." [54]

The strategies were offered in the form of widely distributed booklets, produced with the expectation that the entire department, not just specific pockets of the force, would focus on the highlighted issues and solutions. All NYPD units would be judged on their contributions to crime reduction. Comparisons would be made between efforts and results; successes could be updated and shared.

Buried Bulletins. The Bratton regime knew where it wanted to go and how to get there, but street cops needed more than inspirational messages to "climb on board." Focus groups were seen as the key. For two months, several ranks (for example, patrol officers and sergeants) and positions (for example, platoon commanders and special operations lieutenants) took part in weekly meetings at headquarters.

Despite some fears in high command that the groups would turn into gripe sessions, they provided useful sounding boards for the rank and file. Perhaps not surprisingly, the sessions delivered messages that were unfit for public consumption. According to John Linder, the management consultant who guided the meetings, the street cops saw a wide chasm separating them from the official hierarchy. They wanted to be active in fighting crime; instead, the bureaucracy pressed them to issue parking summonses, meet quotas, curb overtime, avoid trouble, and clear the 911 backlog. Ground patrol's obvious distrust of the top echelon was expressed in such telling statements as "This place is not on the level."[55] The focus groups identified, in consultant terms, "underactivated values in an organization," which needed to be linked "to the purposes of a strong leader."[56] In police language: "The cops had to buy in." The focus groups legitimized the direction of the new police regime.

That was not all they accomplished. Focus groups were a convenient camouflage for information gathering. By gaining the trust of the focus groups, the police hierarchy could uncover what was really going on in the field. A case in point was one focus group with special operations lieutenants (SOLs). As key assistants to precinct commanders, the SOLs knew the inside workings of their precincts. Much to their surprise, after their focus group complained that they did not have enough mobile digital terminals, a problem that hampered criminal identification, they soon received the terminals. (Mobile digital terminals can immediately display motor vehicle registration and licensing information, as well as outstanding criminal court warrants.) "It was amazing," recalls one SOL. "Here our requests had been bouncing around at 1PP [One Police Plaza] for months." The SOLs were now ready to believe. Their focus group unearthed buried bones: what and who worked or did not work. Armed with this inside information gleaned from the SOLs, the high command could ask more pointed questions when it came time to interrogate precinct commanders.

Independent reports pumped up NYPD managerial claims. The Harvard Business School, for example, proclaimed that reengineering "eliminated a reporting level."[57] Gone were the divisional commanders who stood between the precinct commanders and their borough commanders. Or so it appeared. But as one top commander put it, this "flattening" of the hierarchical pyramid was largely "fluff." The number of commanders serving in these borough positions shrunk, but the individuals were not discharged. They worked under new titles—"adjutant" and "administrator." Furthermore, the decision to reduce the number of divisional commanders was never discussed during reengineering. The new regime had resolved, at the very outset, to trim the organization. Reengineering provided the spin; outsiders recycled the tale.

The real purpose of eliminating the divisional command level, however, was to free up higher positions for precinct commanders, most of whom had traditionally held the rank of captain.

Ten additional deputy inspector positions, the rank above captain, were now open for precinct commanders of so-called "B" (middle) level crime precincts. Nine more inspector positions, the rank above deputy inspectors, were freed up for "A" (high) level crime precinct commanders. Freshly empowered precinct commanders, the linchpins of the NYPD's newly dispersed authority, now had broader career paths and incentives to do well.

Conclusion

The Giuliani mayoral campaign and the first several months of the new administration ushered in a period of intense reform efforts. Leaders skilled in the use of mass media and cognizant of the dynamics of team building communicated tangible directions for the NYPD. Personnel known for their activist skills were promoted over those with more seniority. From now on, it was claimed, the nature of crime problems, not existing organizational arrangements, would dictate strategies. For example, drugs and guns were found to exist in overlapping geographic patterns. That realization resulted in the initial replacement of specialized drug units with Street Narcotics and Gun (SNAG) Units, which conducted aggressive, round-the-clock, buy-and-bust activities against gun and drug dealers in targeted locations. Street cop morale was raised through symbolic gestures such as new uniforms, command visits, and committee involvement.

The reengineering and new strategies documents represented a systematic plunge through the layers of bureaucracy that had stymied previous attempts at innovation. As daring and refreshing as this multilevel approach was, there remained the danger that innovations would be short-lived and would thrive only in localized pockets of the NYPD. Nagging questions persisted. How could these efforts become more than a rearrangement of organizational furniture? What is to prevent historic resistance to decentralization from prevailing? The road to NYPD reform was littered with abandoned pilot projects. How would the top brass make sure that all commands were adopting the agreed-upon strategies? The answers lay in a development that no one envisioned at the outset, and that received far less initial publicity than other reforms. Its name was Compstat, and it developed into the new policing's major propellant and centerpiece.

5 ENTER COMPSTAT

"Is anyone going to take ownership of this case?" bellows Chief of Department Louis Anemone from one end of a long rectangular table. Standing at the other end of the table are the precinct commanding officer (CO) and his key associates. Anemone is refering to a month-long series of robberies with striking resemblances to robberies in an adjoining precinct.

"We are getting on top of it," replies the precinct CO.

"What is the plan to go after this?" demands Deputy Commissioner Jack Maple.

"The RIP [robbery unit] is looking at this," says the CO.

Anemone commands, "Let's hear from RIP. Look at the overhead map and graph showing most of the robberies occurring after school hours near three subway stops where we have scores of kites [public complaints about drugs]."

"We are aware of this, Chief," replies the RIP sergeant.

"Then why are we down in narc arrests in these areas?" asks Maple. "And who provides information to narcotics [investigators]? Do we have school yearbooks for more information?"

Anemone continues the questioning: "Where is the anticrime unit? There's slippage between robbery squads and precinct teams. We all have ownership of good and bad things. We go to a lot of trouble tracking crime—let's put the resources [to work] to address it. I want you all to get together and have a plan by tomorrow."

This exchange occurred in the "war room," the large Command and Control Center at police headquarters, at a 7:00 A.M. crime strategy meeting in July 1995. Present from a preselected police patrol borough was every precinct and special unit commander for that sector of the city. They were there to assume ownership of crime control, answering to the NYPD's top command.

"Taking ownership" commands great attention at the semiweekly Compstat meetings. (The name *Compstat* arose from "Compare Stats," a computer file name, and not, as is commonly thought, from an abbreviated version of "computer statistics.") In policing, as in the act of dwelling, ownership is more likely to induce action than is tenancy. Some police are committed to the job, and others are just renting space. "Empty suits," the police call them. But assuming ownership is often a slow process. When, in the late summer of 1994, a Queens precinct commander atypically reported, "*I* have four robberies," Anemone, a lead questioner, was delighted. His satisfaction came not from the robberies but from the captain's acknowledgment of ownership. "That's exactly right," said the chief.

Before Compstat, most precinct commanders did not see crime reduction as their foremost responsibility. In addition, COs were essentially on their own in combating crime. Some did well; many did not. The department wasn't equipped to assist or motivate COs to attack crime and disorder problems. Headquarters wasn't tracking crime trends in the precincts or evaluating CO performance in fighting crime. Detective bureaus and other specialty units worked in isolation and sometimes at cross-purposes with precinct patrol commanders. The department was extremely slow to allocate resources and personnel to emerging or growing problems in the precincts.

Anemone's praise of the young Queens precinct captain for

assuming ownership of robberies sent a message to the entire department—ownership is key to command accountability and recognition. Not only will the high command hold the front lines accountable, but street captains themselves must be committed to ownership. In November 1994, Kevin McBride, a young Queens captain who was alert to Compstat's crime reduction goal, posted officers near his precinct's ATM machines as part of his Christmas holiday crime reduction plan; precincts typically targeted only commercial strips during the holidays. McBride's strategy was an early Compstat example of a CO "thinking outside the box." Ownership begets creativity and advancement. The captain was subsequently promoted and transferred to a more desirable precinct.

Enforcing accountability and improving the crime-fighting ratio of "full suit" to "empty suits" required updated crime information, graphic crime mapping, revised crime strategies, empowered precinct commanders, street-level creative problem solving, and breached unit barriers. Compstat emerged as the catalyst and arena for these developments.

Origins

During the early months of his administration, Commissioner William Bratton called for a weekly, one-on-one current events briefing with a representative from each of the NYPD's eight bureaus. Deputy Commissioner Maple authorized the head of the Patrol Bureau to discuss crime statistics with the commissioner. A disturbing reality surfaced: The NYPD did not know its current crime statistics. There was a reporting time lag of three to six months. This news was met with incredulity by Bratton, Maple, and the other top brass who were new to the department. They were even more shocked when some headquarters offices revealed they were rarely able to produce up-to-date crime reports.

Maple, in conjunction with Chief Patrick Kelleher, executive officer of the Patrol Bureau's office, and Kelleher's key staff members, Lieutenant William Gorta and Sergeant John Yohe, pressed the precincts to generate crime activity statistics on a weekly basis. During the second week of February 1994, all precincts provided a hand count of the seven major crimes for the first six weeks of 1993 compared to the same period in 1994. The Patrol Bureau's staff computerized this crime activity and assembled it into a document referred to as the "Compstat book." The first Compstat book included current data on a year-to-date basis for crime complaints and arrests for every major felony category, as well as gun arrests. The data were compiled on citywide, patrol borough, and precinct levels. When it was discovered that some of the arrest statistics were inaccurate, precinct commanders were made accountable for all errors. Elevating the level of responsibility for gathering crime statistics from a clerical task to an administrative obligation signaled that there was a new regime in town.

When he was still chief of patrol, Anemone had direct operational command over all the precincts. With Anemone's supervision and the backing of Chief Kelleher and Deputy Commissioner Maple, the core group, as Gorta put it, "had the juice to make it work." Sergeant Gene Whyte, a key staff member, explained the situation this way: "When the first Compstat book was shipped to precinct commanders, it was like a bill. The price for being a commander was to do something about the crime in your area." From that point forward, the Compstat book became more accurate as arrests were downloaded directly from the NYPD's On-Line Booking System (OLBS).

A key to the development of Compstat was the staff's continuous enhancement and refinement of precinct activity and crime data. That work was first performed in 1994 by individuals reporting to Chief of Patrol Anemone. In 1995 they moved with Anemone when he was promoted to chief of department. Early

Compstat books detailed weekly changes in rates of reported crime and made comparisons among precincts. The third Compstat book noted the "top ten" precincts with the greatest crime increases and those with the greatest decreases (weekly and monthly) by percentage. Similar ratings were given on a monthly and a yearly basis by percentage and in absolute numbers. Later Compstat books provided sixteen pages of rankings by all commands, or precincts, for the week, month, and year, categorized for all major crimes—murder, rape, robbery, felony assault, burglary, grand larceny, and grand larceny auto.[1] In addition, the number of arrests in each precinct were presented for the seven major crimes. These figures were viewed as indicators of patrol effectiveness. Rankings spurred analysis of precinct activities, crime trends, and results and drove commanders to perform better. The March 1994 data would prove crucial to Compstat's evolution from a book of vital crime statistics to an arena in which, depending on the results of their crime strategies, COs would be rewarded or punished.

Launching the Process

Regularly scheduled Compstat meetings grew out of a need for a mechanism to ensure precinct COs' accountability and improve performance. In April 1994, Maple and Anemone were searching for ways to sharpen the NYPD's crime-fighting focus. At that time, for example, boroughs held monthly field robbery meetings in which precinct COs and robbery and anticrime sergeants met with the borough staffs (to whom they reported) to discuss robbery trends. Robbery, in the words of one former top police official, was considered a "bellwether crime, but there was no forum for analysis and coordinated action. Each unit, such as transit, patrol, and housing, had its own way of attacking and recording burglaries." Discussions primarily concentrated on the number of robberies in various commands, not on patterns.

Recalling his days as a young cop, Deputy Chief Pat Devlin remembered the response of his precinct CO when asked by the borough why robbery had increased in his precinct: "Sometimes robbery goes up, and sometimes it goes down!"

Top-level executives requested that the Brooklyn North Patrol Borough hold one of its monthly robbery meetings at headquarters—One Police Plaza. The precinct commanders and others were nervous because they did not know what to expect from the top brass. After the Brooklyn borough CO's overview of special conditions, several precinct COs were called to the front of the room. Their presentations, although suitable for public community-council meetings, lacked in-depth analyses of complex crime problems. Dissatisfied, Anemone abruptly terminated the meeting and announced monthly meetings at headquarters for each borough. The process was launched; there was no turning back.

Different formats for these monthly meetings were tried by Chief Kelleher and his staff, particularly Sergeant Gene Whyte. The press room seating arrangement was shifted from rows to a horseshoe shape to encourage more interaction. The issue, according to the chief, was clear: "What are you doing about crime?" COs were asked. Later meetings were moved to the more prestigious and imposing but underutilized Command and Control Center.[2]

At a typical headquarters meeting, the top brass are seated in swivel chairs at a long table lit by green desk lamps. Maple and Anemone, the lead inquisitors, sit at the center of the table behind a large computer monitor. A telephone is linked to a high-tech console that flashes charts, maps, and graphs onto three huge video screens. Everyone tends to be on edge. Precinct commanders and their staffs are interrogated as they stand before a lectern under the video screens.

Late in April 1994, the NYPD leadership decided to use the headquarters meetings to link newly released drug and gun strategies with the Compstat books. Tenacity was essential. According to Kelleher, "We knew that we could not afford to miss one month in this operation. Otherwise, the department would not take it seriously, like other [previous] efforts."

The Compstat meetings, held Wednesday and Friday mornings, became mandatory. They began promptly at 7:00 A.M., when there were likely to be few distractions. Departmental big shots could not delegate this assignment, since their work days generally begin at 10:00 A.M.

Mapping Crime

Intensified crime fighting was not contingent only on routine strategy meetings, crime analysis, and timely and accurate information. Data had to be portrayed clearly and in a format that could be acted on quickly. The key was to provide departmentwide access to crime location details. Some precincts had sporadically maintained simple pin maps to record where robberies occurred. But the maps had low priority. Civilians did the plotting, and many precinct commanders rarely used the information when deciding where to deploy their anticrime units. Besides, the NYPD did not mandate the use of maps. Therefore, the prevailing assumption was that they were not that important.

Maple asked the Compstat Office, as it was now called, to pin-map all robberies, shootings, grand larcenies, and murders within East New York—a high-crime Brooklyn precinct (the 75th).[3] This directive was issued at the same time that regular headquarters Compstat meetings were starting. The practicality of pin-mapping quickly became apparent when Martin O'Boyle, then chief of the Narcotics Division, used the 75th Precinct crime maps to redeploy his street narcotics and gun teams from their original target zones to high-profile hot spots. At about the same time, a Queens precinct CO appeared at a Compstat meeting with a primitive pin map of crime in his command. Chief Anemone latched onto this and ordered all precincts to maintain pin maps, cover them with acetate overlays for each of the major index crimes, and bring them to Compstat meetings. Pin-mapping was now part of the furniture.

As computer capabilities improved at headquarters and at precincts, pin maps were replaced by overlay maps created by crime-mapping computer software. The new maps showing crime activity in the city were displayed on large video screens. The computer-made maps included narcotics complaints; time, day of week, and location of crime events; and information regarding police deployment and arrest activity. Later Compstats recorded and mapped the times and places of precinct shootings and their relationship to drug-dealing sites. A powerful software tool, MapInfo 94, became the NYPD's crime radar screen, with attention-grabbing colors and shapes. Red dots indicated drug complaints from the public, blue dots showed drug arrests, green triangles represented shooting incidents, and yellow dots indicated homicides. When projected on the war room's large overhead screen and on small individual screens, the overlays of colors superimposed on street locations were impressive.[4] For the first time, all the crime and arrest data that were previously floating in the vast NYPD universe were brought together through the convergence of Compstat books and crime strategy meetings. The stars and planets were in alignment; crime information was easy to read and digest.

Information exploded. Some correlations, which were previously suspected, were demonstrated: Homicides' yellow dots mingled with drug complaints' red dots. Gun arrests' blue squares, added to the number of desk appearance tickets (DATs), helped track quality-of-life arrests. (DATs are given for minor misdemeanors, such as drinking beer on the street, littering, and squeegeeing. Rather than tie up the criminal justice system with arrests, police have traditionally given DATs to people who sup-

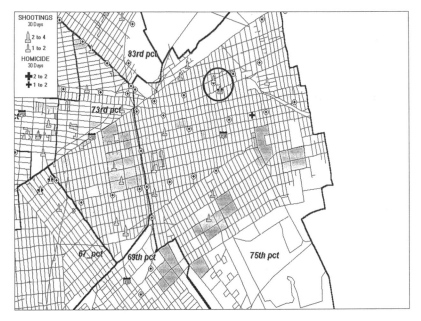

Compstat crime mapping.

posedly have ties to the community and will honor the DATs and show up in court.)

Late in 1994, the Compstat Office analyzed the on-line booking system to determine how many officers had not effected an arrest during the year. The results were shocking: 28 percent of Queens cops, for example, had not produced an arrest in the first half of the year. This information was conveyed to Queens precinct patrol leaders at a headquarters Compstat meeting. As it turned out, they had little knowledge of their cops' arrest activities. The story was leaked to the press and appeared on page one of the *Daily News*. Since then, arrest pie charts have regularly been generated as another stimulus to police activity and a gauge of crime strategy effectiveness. On the back of each precinct pie chart is a listing of its officers and their arrest numbers. The charts show what percentage of the precinct is making the bulk of the arrests, thus pinpointing commands with an inor-

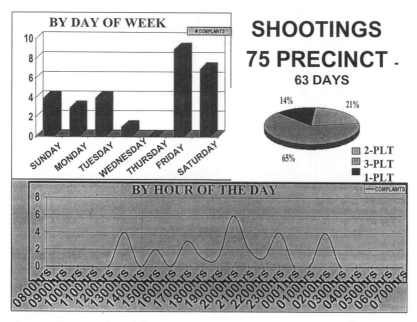

Compstat crime breakdowns.

dinate number of unmotivated officers (or a low crime rate). This information is provided to each precinct CO for review and action.[5]

Qualitative Information

As the Compstat meetings evolved, the top level of the NYPD sought not only more quantitative information about crime complaints, arrests, patterns, and trends, but also qualitative information about precinct and community conditions and their relationship to effective crime fighting. In May 1994, for example, informal meetings were held between Maple and all precinct special operations lieutenants (SOLs), one borough at a time. This activity was related to the focus groups that met over a period of two months (see Chapter 4). The idea was not to criticize the SOLs, but to gain their confidence and find out what was going on in their commands. Because most SOLs were the officers who were most familiar with precinct crime strategies, they were an excellent source of information to arm the higher echelons for subsequent formal Compstat meetings.

In October 1994, Bratton requested a sheet for each precinct that showed a photo of the CO and provided information about his or her activities and performance. This was a major undertaking for Kelleher and others in the Patrol Bureau because the information was scattered throughout the NYPD. The resulting document, the precinct commander profile, provided information about appointment date and years in rank, education and specialized training, most recent performance evaluation, and previous command positions. Since 1994, the profiles have expanded to include community demographics, crime statistics, summons activity, available resources, average response time for the delivery of services, domestic violence incidents, unfounded radio runs, and officer absences. These last two items are believed to be an important indicator of command morale. Commissioner Howard Safir added integrity monitoring to the list to convey the importance of citizen complaints and charges of brutality and misconduct.[6]

From the very beginning, commander profiles have been instrumental in enhancing accountability. Now regularly distributed at all Compstat meetings, profiles enable the top brass easily to match a face with performance. Bratton first used profiles in the fall of 1994, when he decided which COs would remain, move, or be promoted. Between 1995 and 1996, profiles were developed for detective squad commanders, robbery unit supervisors, borough commanding officers, narcotics supervisors, Housing Bureau supervisors, and Transit Bureau supervisors.

These supervisory profiles help the upper echelon evaluate and compare supervisors when making promotion and transfer decisions. The material is also increasingly geared to specific unit operations. For example, investigative profiles of detectives and members of narcotics units furnish information about arrest activities, caseloads and clearances, the number and ranks of assigned personnel, their absence rates, and the number of perpetrator debriefings and search warrants executed. Narcotics supervisor profiles also specify registered confidential informants, long-term buy operations, and narcotics activity intelligence reports received, investigated, and closed.

A March 1998 Compstat meeting illustrated the usefulness of commander profiles. Deputy Commissioner Edward Norris congratulated a narcotics supervisor for his unit's remarkable arrest activity. "Your record is consistently good," remarked Norris. "We want you to know we appreciate this." The supervisor replied, "Thank you, boss. We try hard." At that point, Commissioner Safir examined the supervisor's profile sheet and matched the photo with the face standing at the front of the room. He nodded approvingly; it was not long before the supervisor was promoted.

The quest for qualitative information continues. Beginning in 1996, photos of precinct areas taken at peak crime activity times have been displayed at some Compstat meetings. For example, photos might show precinct conditions during hours when panhandlers are prohibited from loitering near ATM machines. If photos reveal deteriorating conditions, such as drug activity or loitering, the times of the day when the photos were taken are compared with the times when narcotics and patrol officers work and arrest violators. Immediate attention is given to the problem (in this case, how officer schedules differ from crime patterns), and remedies are planned.

Compstat Compliance

Compstat is NYPD's response to the former police commissioner Lee Brown's 1991 lament that the vast size of the department makes sharing information an uphill battle. It "is so large," Brown noted in the introduction to his ambitious community policing reform program (see Chapter 3), "that many units do not have the opportunity to interact with other units on a regular basis."[7] Compstat gathers all NYPD informational arrows in one quiver, targeting crime conditions for all key decision makers at their crime-fighting meetings. Interaction and information sharing are now built into the system. The top brass convene to discuss crime on a regular basis, and the scheduled crime strategy meetings engage both top echelon and each borough's precinct COs once every four or five weeks. These built-in interactions are a major departure from previous practice. Before Compstat, observed CO Jane Perlov of Northern Manhattan's active 30th Precinct, a CO would have to plow through "millions of layers" to speak to the chief of department, chief of detectives, chief of Organized Crime Control, or the police commissioner. "It is an incredible thing. We [now] see them on a regular basis at headquarters." Inspector Perlov, an accomplished law enforcement manager and Compstat performer, does not necessarily enjoy the demanding Compstat preparation time, yet she recognizes that the benefits outweigh the drawbacks. Deputy Inspector Vincent DeMarino, a capable Brooklyn precinct CO noted, "I am able to get answers to some of my questions. They [the top brass] know me here at Compstat. We are more and more on the same wavelength."

Memories and Meetings

Compstat provides the arena for airing sharpened department-wide crime strategies. But in a department dominated by disconnected agendas, tactical fidelity to grand plans is not assured. A weak link in Compstat's armor was the absence of an institutional record of field plans and performance before 1995. At first, an assessment of how well the NYPD was complying with Compstat decisions depended on the memories of two individuals: Maple and Anemone. Maple felt there was no need to record

Compstat decisions for subsequent meetings. "I will remember the material at later meetings," he observed. And what if he was not present at a later meeting? Maple replied, "Then Anemone will remember it." The value of maintaining a record of Compstat meetings was not appreciated at the outset.

Within the next several months, however, it became apparent that innovation could not rest solely on the dynamism and memories of a few key individuals, no matter how energetic and committed they were. Compstat was yielding a torrent of information and myriad decisions that demanded documentation and follow-up. Consequently, as the number of crime-fighting strategies increased, the need for institutional memory and compliance mechanisms became more obvious. As Chief Anemone recalled, "We were giving direction at the Compstat meetings, but we didn't always see follow-through, and some claimed conclusions that hadn't been reached. We told them that we will have minutes, and everyone will critique them after the meeting."

Beginning in the spring of 1996, Compstat staff in the chief of department's office began taking detailed minutes. Major issues requiring follow-up and resolution now are identified in an abbreviated or summarized version of the minutes, which is promptly distributed to top-level officials. Convening immediately after each Compstat meeting, this group of high-ranking officers reviews the summarized minutes and assigns responsibility for solutions and implementation.

These post-Compstat meetings became standard after an erroneous leak to the press claimed that Compstat was requiring all units to schedule the bulk of their personnel to be on duty in the middle of the night. Post-Compstat meetings provide an official record and ensure that everyone is "on the same page," a critical chore since selective leaking to the press—a time-honored method for advancing the interests of department units—is unlikely to cease. Compstat does not dissolve internal rivalry, but it brings much of it out in the open, on the department's main playing field. And when there are genuine misunderstandings, they can more readily be resolved in this official setting.

Post-Compstat meetings have satisfactorily dealt with the problem of mistaking tips for official policies. A *tip* occurs when, for instance, a high-level official tells a precinct commander what he did when he was a commander—such as send his warrant squad out at 6:00 A.M. to search the homes of those wanted for ignoring court orders. Although such advice is not necessarily intended to be acted on by all precincts, some tips have been perceived as official departmental policy. A *policy* is something the department wants everyone to do. If, for example, there are shootings in a neighborhood, anyone picked up for questioning must be asked about the whereabouts of guns in the area.

The summary minutes of Compstat meetings provide valuable insights. Nettlesome exchanges may highlight areas that need improvement. For example, there are requests for written reports of oral Compstat presentations, information that is properly entered on reports, tactical follow-through, appropriate personnel deployment, and greater coordination among units. Other issues, such as accurate reporting, generate a host of directives, for example, the following: "CO SAT-COM (Head Brooklyn North Patrol Borough) to provide copy of detective/narcotics operation presentation to Chief Anemone." When a disparity between headquarters and field information is uncovered at a Compstat meeting, it triggers a directive, such as: "73 Precinct narcotics supervisor to review profile for accuracy for next Compstat."

During an August 1996 Compstat meeting, the gravity of improper informational reporting became apparent when a Brooklyn detective commander was questioned about his handling of a homicide case that arose during a drug war. The groups involved rode bicycles while shooting. Chief Anemone and Deputy Commissioner Edward Norris (who had replaced Maple) held the detective's feet to the fire. "Was the witness interviewed?" inquired Anemone. "An attempt was made to interview her," replied the detective, "but so far she has not been located." "Then why is this information not in the file folder?" queried Norris as he examined his records. Chief Anemone agreed: "If it is not in the case folder, it does not exist. Don't put the information in a separate book." This exchange produced a directive in the minutes to the "Chief of Detectives—to ensure negative results be documented on DD 5's [follow-up investigative reports] and put in case folders." General directives often originate from specific instances uncovered at Compstat meetings because the top brass is convinced that if a deficiency exists in one police sector, it is likely to occur elsewhere.

Many Compstat minutes stress enforcement compliance and follow-through. The following example illustrates how unresolved crimes or pending issues are tagged for future reporting: "88 Precinct RIP [robbery] CO identified a loosely knit violent gang/group in 88 Precinct—approximately 12 persons—2 of the 12 are wanted. Update at next Compstat meeting of enforcement." A week later, the minutes included a directive to "CO 73 Precinct—as per Chief of Detectives—to review methadone clinics within precinct for possible connection in robberies. Update at next meeting."

Rather than waiting until the next Compstat meeting, details concerning urgent situations are often due the next day, as indicated in the following minutes: "CO Intelligence Division—to have report on circumstance of assault case in the 90 Precinct and incident in 72 Precinct regarding the Latin Kings and the Wild Chicanos. To be endorsed by Chief of Detectives and delivered to Chief of Department (Chief Materasso) no later than Thursday, August 7, 1997."

Effective resource deployment and unit coordination are more complex issues: "CO Borough Narcotics—Correct the lack of arrests after 0100 hours in the 60 Precinct. Update at next Compstat meeting." Another meeting resulted in this directive:

"CO Patrol Borough Brooklyn South/CO Brooklyn Robbery Squad—Pay special attention to the robberies along the train lines. Appropriate resources to be allocated." These directives allow higher echelons to reinforce their views about specific operational strategies and tactics.

Compstat frequently produces directives calling for multiunit strikes against violence. For instance, the following directive requests three divisions to focus on repeat domestic violence offenders: "Chief of Patrol, Housing Bureau, Chief of Detectives, CO SATCOM (Brooklyn North)—Domestic violence cases must be closely monitored on high propensity cases. Persons on high propensity list who have active cases or warrants should be top priority for apprehension. All housing, patrol, and detective personnel should be aware of persons on high propensity list. Ensure all services are provided to victims of domestic violence (re: relocation, home visits, etc.)."

The most recurrent theme, even of those minutes that deal with success, is follow-up and reinforcement. Units are pushed to emulate successful tactics disclosed at Compstat meetings. A September 1997 meeting, for example, revealed a high payoff when the Brooklyn Housing Bureau checked up on outstanding warrants of individuals receiving C (criminal court) summonses. This tactic was consistent with the NYPD's assault on quality-of-life offenses (see Chapter 4). The NYPD first addressed this issue with DATs and now was adding the C summons as another tool. Predictably, this was the Compstat follow-up question: Were other police units also consistently running warrants on their C summons recipients? Thus the minutes' reference: "Commissioner Norris—To check the running of warrants on C summonses. Housing Checks indicate a 10- to 12-percent hit ratio." Similarly, when a 75th Precinct robbery supervisor experienced considerable tactical success, the minutes recorded requests for emulation elsewhere. In this case, "75 RIP [robbery] sergeant—Changes tour of personnel for specific operations and is doing excellent job in warrant-card enforcement. CO SAT-COM [Patrol Borough Brooklyn North] to ensure all RIP/Squads to follow this procedure."

Pre-Compstat Preparation

Whereas minutes and post-Compstat meetings were later developments, pre-Compstat preparations have been thorough from the outset. Yet, here, too, there has been an evolution from informal, oral overviews to more systematic, in-depth briefings. Preparations for meetings first centered on statistical reviews of crime, precinct by precinct. The Compstat meeting timetable scheduled precincts by patrol borough, with the expectation that eight to twelve precincts would be represented at every meeting. It quickly became apparent, however, that only three to five precinct commanders could be adequately questioned at a typical Compstat session. Briefings became more selective and concentrated as precinct presentations were streamlined, crime data mushroomed, and Compstat staff became more familiar with precinct problems.

In 1995, the Compstat staff began supplementing its oral briefings to Maple and Anemone with increasingly refined briefing books. These books summarize each precinct's unresolved investigations and patterns of criminal activity, particularly homicides, shootings, rapes, and robberies.

Unresolved serious criminal incidents are prominently profiled and usually lead off a precinct report. The following November 1996 homicide report ends with a specific note as to how the department is working to apprehend the killer: "[Name] M/B/20 was shot to death while standing in front of [address]. He was arrested 6 times for robbery, grand larceny, drugs, and assault. He was a target narcotic violator and would have been on probation until 8/1/98. There are 100 Nitro hits [positive identification on narcotics computer system] and 16 kites [public complaints of drug exchanges] on his residence address. There are 3 Nitro hits and 2 kites on the location of occurrence. PDS [precinct detective squad] has identified the perp as [Name]. It is believed that [Name] has fled the state, and the squad is working with outside agencies to locate him."

A 1996 homicide report updates Compstat participants by adding the results of lie-detector tests conducted after an August Compstat meeting: "[Name] F/H/47, was found DOA [dead on arrival] lying face up on the floor of her bedroom, with a gunshot wound to her right temple. She was found by her son [Name]. She had no criminal record. There are 2 Nitro hits on the location of occurrence, which is her residence [address]. PDS believes victim's son is responsible for this homicide. He was scheduled for a polygraph on 8/26/96, and he passed. Victim's boyfriend was polygraphed, and the results were inconclusive."

The briefing books arm Compstat interrogators with up-to-date information. For example, "[Complaint number] Wednesday 6/5/96 1810 hours [Name] M/B/45 was stabbed to death in a bodega at [address]. He used 7 aliases. He was arrested 7 times for robbery, burglary, drugs, weapons, and assault. He had 7 driver's license suspensions. He violated parole, and a warrant was issued on 4/18/96. There is 1 Nitro hit on his residence address and 1 kite on the location of occurrence. PDS states witnesses heard an argument; victim pulled knife and perp pulled gun."

Here's another report: "[Complaint number] 12/02/96 F/B/30 Stranger [rape]. The victim states while walking in the street, she was approached by a M/B/35 driving a small white car. He brandished a gun and ordered her to get in his car. Her hands were tied behind her back, and she was blindfolded. She was taken to an unknown house where she was raped. SVS [Special Victims Squad] states complainant's story is inconsistent. Medical report negative." As this brief follow-up report illustrates, Compstat keeps everyone in the loop as the department explores an alleged crime.

Crime clusters and patterns also are featured in briefing books. The following incidents of purse snatching have several common threads, and so do the drugstore thefts described in the next paragraph. "Pattern #41—Five Incidents: Two in the 61 Pct., two in the 66 Pct., and one in the 62 Pct. One M/B, 25–33 years, 5'11" 6'02", 170–190 lbs., follows victim into lobby, hallway, or to apartment door. Perp then grabs victim from rear, demanding bag, and pushes victim to floor. Victims are all Caucasian elderly females in their 70s or 80s."

"Pattern #57—Three Incidents: One in the 62 Pct., one in the 63 Pct., and one in the 104 Pct. One M/B, 25 years of age, 5'7", 145 lbs., wearing a jogging jacket. The perpetrator enters Rite Aid Pharmacies and displays a gun. Victims are forcibly taken to the location of the safe and USC [U.S. currency] is removed. To prevent pursuit, victims are then forced to undress before the perpetrators flee. On two occasions, the victims were struck with weapons."

Briefing books, besides sketching ongoing detective investigations, remind participants that they are expected to follow up on suggestions and leads. The following requests for information grew out of the absence of arrests after 6 P.M. and the presence of a heroin-dealing gang: "CO P.B.M.N. [Patrol Borough Manhattan North] Narco—Last meeting we discussed the fact that there were no arrests after 1800 hours in the 23rd Precinct. You also mentioned a Cuban-run gang/organization selling heroin at 110th St. and Lexington. Update?"

"CO Manhattan Detectives—Last meeting we discussed the 23rd Precinct homicide [Date and complaint number] [street number] Madison Ave. The Squad said a possible perp is [Name]. Also said this may be a drug-gang killing. They are selling black top crack. [Vials of crack, depending on the variety, have different colored covers. The color is often used as a distinguishing mark for merchandising purposes.] We asked that the Boro CO ensures that the 23rd pct squad has a comprehensive plan to apprehend the perps wanted in the homicides at [two street addresses on] Madison Ave. Update?"

"First Degree Sex Crimes [complaint number] 4/28/96 F/H/22 Acquaintance Rape. Perp went to victim's house and forcibly raped her. PDS states perp is identified, and they are looking for him. A wanted card has been issued. How are they looking for him? Human Resource checked for Public Assistance?"

The torrent of prepared follow-up questions at the end of the following minutes typifies the intensity of a grilling at a Compstat meeting. "Victim Profiles: [complaint number] 4/18/96 M/W/30 [Name] stabbed to death on Queens Plaza subway platform at 0100 hrs. after having a dispute with a companion. [Name of victim] was arrested 21 times for burglary, assault, robbery, CPCS [criminal possession of controlled substance], and criminal mischief. There are 12 Nitro hits on his residence address and one kite. How many canvasses were done? Interviews of conductors, train operators, porters, clerks, N/B-S/B side of station? Has the companion been identified? Any witnesses?"

Briefing books were at first prepared only for the chief of department, deputy commissioner for crime control strategies, and police commissioner. Although bureau chiefs attended meetings and occasionally participated, their involvement was originally less central to the questioning process. Eventually, these chiefs (chief of detectives, organized crime control, transit, and housing, plus the first deputy commissioner) became more involved and were also provided with briefing books.

Constant Compstat

By honoring its 1994 decision to hold Compstat meetings on a regular basis, the NYPD has helped to ensure accountability. Precincts know they will be queried about performance and results every four or five weeks. Nevertheless, there was a concern, several years ago, that some precincts were slacking off because of the predictable Compstat schedule. Thus, in the summer of 1995 Commissioner Safir switched off Compstat's automatic pilot by killing the established schedule. Precincts and boroughs now learn only a few days prior to a scheduled meeting whether they will be requested to appear.

Generally, precinct scheduling is based on unfavorable crime statistics or sudden upturns in particular crimes or shootings—known by the NYPD as "spikes." The weekly spike report, developed in mid-1996, is an outgrowth of the early 1994 Compstat precinct rankings. These published reports list all precincts, ranking them according to weekly, monthly, and yearly increases in crime. The seven major crimes mentioned earlier, as well as shooting incidents and gun arrests, are tracked.

In addition to the spike reports, the following considerations may be taken into account when precincts are selected for Compstat meetings: Which crimes are rising most rapidly? Are these crimes associated with other crimes? How many weeks has a precinct been undergoing spikes? How long has it been since the precinct last appeared at a Compstat meeting? Precincts and their boroughs also become alert to these considerations and try to predict their next "calling"—sometimes successfully, sometimes not. This "subject to be called" approach keeps precincts on their toes and constantly reinforces the primary importance of crime reduction. If a precinct's shootings continue to climb, for example, its leaders can be recalled the following week. One entire borough's crime rate rose so quickly in early 1998 that the borough was present at two consecutive meetings—a first in Compstat's history. At the same time, *all* headquarters and field units connected with borough and precinct activities must be present at Compstat meetings, further emphasizing shared responsibilities.

PIMs and Patterns

Compstat not only gathers, reformats, and compares department-wide information, it also reinvigorates its flow. During an August 1995 Compstat meeting, for example, it became clear to two Compstat staff members that the borough robbery squads were unable to share information about robbery patterns occurring in different precincts within the same borough. Therefore, Compstat personnel developed the idea of a pattern identification module (PIM), or unit, for each borough. A PIM is composed of representatives of the housing, transit, patrol, detective, and organized crime control bureaus, and the robbery squad.

Anemone and Maple backed the idea despite initial resistance from the Detective Bureau, which considered crime pattern identification to be within its province. Almost immediately, an NYPD order required borough modules to be established by mid-September. The modules' assignments were extensive: Review daily index crime reports and narcotics complaints; immediately notify borough commanders of sharp increases in violent crimes so that necessary resources can be allocated; identify patterns, trends, or clusters by crime method and location, and then notify detective, housing, and narcotics units and others; discern possible patterns through crime-mapping; keep track of perpetrator descriptions for possible similarities or identification in other precincts; and confer with counterparts in other boroughs regarding possible patterns or trends and wanted or arrested perpetrators.

Alert precinct commanders now draw on their borough PIMs for additional information about precinct crime patterns and clusters. For example, a late 1995 Brooklyn South Patrol Borough PIM "Flash Notification" informed all borough patrol officers of the following robbery pattern: "The Brooklyn Robbery Squad has identified a pattern of robberies occurring in the vicinity of the Sheepshead Houses, located in the confines of the 61st Precinct. In all incidents the perpetrators used physical force." The notification listed the ten crime complaint numbers and the robbery addresses, and then gave a description of the suspect, which turned out to be instrumental in his apprehension.

The more energetic boroughs and their precincts see a PIM's communication as a "heads up," a way to anticipate the next move by headquarters. They well remember August 1995, when the PIMs' supervisory sergeants were called to headquarters to meet with Anemone and Maple, who informed them of the importance of the PIMs' mission. It is not often that sergeants meet with high-level brass at headquarters to launch a new initiative.

PIMs have transmitted sophisticated crime information, crossing precinct and even borough boundaries. A March 1996 Brooklyn North Patrol Borough PIM informed its precincts, for example, about the theft of plumbing equipment from company vans: "1st Precinct squad [the detective unit in lower Manhattan] is currently investigating 12 cases of Grand Larceny Auto that have strong similarities. The vehicles . . . are vans belonging to [name of plumbing companies]. These [car company] vans mostly contain large quantities of equipment and plumbing supplies. The vans are usually white or red in color and the vehicle years vary from the early 1980s to 1992.

"The vehicles are being stolen from the confines of the 1st Precinct. Some of the vehicles have been recovered within the confines of the 79, 81, and 88 Precincts [all in Brooklyn North]. All of the vehicles have been recovered without their contents."

This PIM information was key to successfully targeting the van thieves. Before the establishment of PIMs, there were only sporadic efforts to systematically share information about crime patterns that crossed precinct borders within a borough, to say nothing of sharing information among precincts outside a particular borough. The three Brooklyn North precincts in the preceding example are part of a borough with over 800,000 people—

about 12 percent of New York City's population—spread over 23 square miles. Coordination within such a large, congested area is a complex task. In addition to emcompassing a large borough, this remarkable PIM report included information about crime within a precinct across the Brooklyn Bridge, in lower Manhattan (within a different patrol borough—the Manhattan South Borough).

Because of their success, PIMs have gained increasing notice and acceptance. Monitored and now recorded in briefing books, each PIM report is given a number, as illustrated by the following: "Pattern Identification Module PIM #5—Commercial Burglary. Nine incidents involving perps who remove or push in the air conditioning units to gain entry. PIM #5 also in the 104, 109, 110, 114, and 115 Pcts."

"PIM #2—Burglary. A male and female Hispanic with two children use ruse to enter victims' homes. All the victims are senior citizens."

"PIM #10—Robbery. Several incidents in the 75 Pct involving two M/B's impersonating police officers who rob businesses under the ruse of executing a search warrant. Perps display shields and guns. IAB [Internal Affairs Bureau] is also investigating these incidents."

PIMs have developed in an unexpected direction. In addition to monitoring and recording crime patterns, PIMs circulate Compstat messages. PIMs have linked up with borough crime strategists, who became important players in the summer of 1994, as more and more crime tips and creative precinct-problem-solving emerged at meetings. PIM strategists now attend all headquarters Compstat meetings and report back to their respective boroughs about citywide hot topics, strategies, and criminal patterns.

Sergeant Paul Scott, the Brooklyn North crime strategist, attended an April 1996 headquarters Compstat meeting for Queens North. At his borough's local Compstat meeting, which took place after the headquarters meeting, he was able to report that the chief of department was interested in the innovative car checkpoint tactics used in Queens, the advanced organization and training for print dusting done on Staten Island, and aggressive pursuit of credit card fraud through high-level credit card company contacts initiated in Queens.

PIMs are also borough tipsters, playing coach to precinct COs and to members of other bureaus. PIMs not only issue alerts about crime trends and patterns, they also provide a safety service by raising street cops' awareness of dangerous operations (for example, stick-up teams) in their precincts. Compstat and its PIMs offshoot have not replaced the grapevine, but they have become the prime grapes.

There is no quicker way to spread a message about organizational priorities and interests than to raise it at a Compstat meeting. At an October 1996 meeting, Captain Ron Wasson reported the details of the 77th Precinct's creative and successful use of general business law and administrative codes to eliminate storefront drug locations. At the conclusion of the discussion, Anemone commended him: "You give new meaning to the phrase 'problem solving.' Are the other borough crime strategists paying attention?" Sweet or sour, these messages rapidly spread throughout the department.

Unexpectedly, PIMs also have profited the NYPD in a far more fundamental way. When the transit and housing police were consolidated into the NYPD in 1995, adding 6,000 more police to the department by the stroke of a pen, it was unclear how these forces were to be integrated. The PIMs were one of the first organizational units where members of the previously separate departments could mix, which helped with the merger. On the PIMs, these groups had frequent access to one another. Participation in PIM and Compstat meetings was often the debut for transit and housing cops.

Conclusion

Hartford Police Chief Joseph F. Croughwell, Jr., attributes his city's sharp drop in crime to Compstat. It enabled all his department's efforts to "come together."[8] Compstat also received credit during Mayor Giuliani's highly successful 1997 reelection campaign, which featured television ads saluting New York City's crime drop. The ads cited as their statistical source "Compstat: NYPD."

Obviously, Compstat has evolved into playing a much more prominent role in NYPD's assault on crime than was anticipated when it was instituted. Witness the inscription on the ten copies of the original February 1994 Compstat book: "These figures are for internal use only—not to be released to the public or other agencies." Three years later, more than 200 Compstat books were issued weekly to all NYPD units, representatives of the city's district attorneys, probation departments, courts, the State Division of Parole, federal agencies, and numerous outsiders. By September 1997, over 250 visitors representing more than twenty-five countries had attended Compstat meetings.

In 1996, Compstat was one of ten winners of the Innovations in American Government award from the Ford Foundation and Harvard University's Kennedy School of Government. Selected from more than 1,550 applicants, the NYPD received an award of $100,000 to promote replication of exemplary government problem-solving approaches. In May 1997 and 1998, the NYPD sponsored three-day Compstat conferences, each time attracting over 400 attendees, including representatives from more than seventy-five police departments in the United States and other countries. The National Institute of Justice has funded the police departments of Indianapolis, Baltimore, and Prince Georges County (Maryland) to replicate Compstat. Other police agencies, such as those in Boston, Washington, D.C., New Orleans, Broward County (Florida), and Hartford also have established their own Compstat programs. Seattle and Los Angeles are currently implementing Compstat as well.

What started out as a computer file and a book to satisfy crime informational needs has evolved, indeed been reconstructed, into a multifaceted forum for coordinated crime-fighting strategies and accountability. Unlike departmental reengineering, focus groups, restructuring, and crime strategies, Compstat was not planned at the outset. Yet it has emerged as the NYPD's most permanent, far-reaching, and widely imitated innovation. Its strength lies in its adaptability and compliance mechanisms.

Commissioner Safir has called Compstat "a shot of adrenaline to the heart of the NYPD." It relentlessly boosts crime fighting while remolding the department. Ultimately, Compstat's significance lies in its impact beyond the confines of its data and its war room–crime strategy meetings. This innovative process radiates throughout the NYPD as the energizer of strikingly creative decision making at headquarters and in the field, as the next two chapters will show.

6 100 PALMETTO STREET

Day one, yo, growin' all up in the ghetto
Now I'm a weed fiend jettin' the Palmetto.
—Wu-Tang Clan[1]

These lyrics, well known among rap music fans, refer to fast trips to 100 Palmetto Street—a notorious urban row house address that provided Brooklyn and much of New York City with drugs. Customers would often line up their cars around the block to buy marijuana. "It was like a drive-through marijuana site," recalls NYPD lawyer Manny Ramlho.[2] The trade was no secret: Even a February 1997 *Nightline* program spotlighted Palmetto's high-quality drugs. For more than fifteen years, this residential site had been a menace to Brooklyn's Bushwick section. Neighbors feared the drug-infested place and the endless loitering, stoop sitting, littering, urination, and other offenses that accompany drug dealing and use. Complaints to offenders were met with repeated aggravated assaults on the complainers. Then crime and disorder radiating from 100 Palmetto abruptly declined more than 50 percent when the location was closed down in March 1997. Aggravated assaults stopped. "It was as if someone shut off a water faucet," recalled one community member. This success story vividly portrays Compstat's driving role in the NYPD's evolutionary reform.

The Precinct Commander and Compstat

"Compstat," says one former precinct commander, "forces you back to basics—time and location of crimes, persons involved, hours we work, and strategies we use." While affixing responsibility, it "gives you the freedom to develop your own problem-solving approaches."

For Deputy Inspector Thomas Dale, Bushwick's 83rd Precinct commander, 100 Palmetto leapt onto Compstat's radar screen in early 1997, when a shooting occurred in a low-rise housing development across the street. Since homicides and shootings are usually the first issues raised at Compstat meetings, Chief of Department Louis Anemone asked, "What is going on there?" Inspector Dale replied, "Well, there is a drug location across the street."

Dale redoubled his activities at 100 Palmetto. He was open to innovation. While a captain in the Detective Bureau in 1994, Dale had been one of seventeen up-and-coming supervisors selected for the commissioner's Plan of Action Committee. Drawing on the work of the reengineering committees (discussed in Chapter 4), the plan called for a comprehensive attack on crime. "There seems to be a consensus . . . in New York City," the committee observed, "that just as people became tired of war, they have become weary of crime. The New York City Police Department must seize the initiative and act on the consensus cited."[3] The precinct commander, while crucial to this struggle, was in a "difficult position . . . due to ever expanding administrative/ operational demands, top-down edicts, and a lack of systems to reward personnel. This committee's recommendations seek to reverse this situation, declare the autonomy of a precinct commander to run a command, and allow the precinct commander to reap the rewards for success or experience the consequences for failure."[4] Dale took these messages to heart. As precinct commander, he had become one of the Compstat stars. Crime in his precinct fell more than 23 percent from 1995 to 1996. The key, Dale declared, was attacking crime hot spots.

If ever there was a crime hot spot, 100 Palmetto was one. "Neighbors regularly complained to us," Dale later recalled. "It is depressing to see this for years and years. It makes it difficult to get respect back from the community." Dale had tried numerous approaches. 100 Palmetto was the site of more than seven search warrants and seventy-five drug arrests in 1996 alone. Narcotics and uniformed cops were assigned there several days a week. Police checked license numbers and searched cars to discourage customers and to squeeze dealers. Low-level drug dealers—known in the trade as "tissues" because they are easily disposable and replaceable—abounded at 100 Palmetto. "We were at our wit's ends," recalls Dale. The community was angry, and continual police assignments were costly.

The property's owner was probably backed by a drug organization that controlled the area. Dale went to the Brooklyn district attorney, who effectively evicted the occupants. Determined to prevent other drug dealers from reentering the premises, Dale posted two officers outside the building around the clock and contacted the lawyers of the NYPD's Civil Enforcement Unit (CEU) to go after the absentee owner. Nine days later, a court order allowed 100 Palmetto to be boarded up. The hot spot had been cooled off.

Civil Enforcement—Overcoming Hurdles

The swift shutdown of 100 Palmetto represented the culmination of an uphill campaign to use civil litigation to combat crime. The effort began as a pilot program in 1991, when Police Commissioner Lee Brown asked each police unit for contributions to the community-policing program's problem-solving efforts (see Chapter 3). The Legal Bureau responded with its Civil Enforcement Initiative (CEI), implemented by the CEU. The approach rested on using civil law, which involves "two individual parties either or both of whom may be public or private entities. The plaintiff (moving party) is asserting that the defendant has somehow caused him injury and is asking a judge to craft a remedy which will compensate for this damage and return him to a condition as close to his pre-injury condition as possible."[5] The CEU incorporated lawyers into the NYPD's crime control efforts, substantially expanding the quality and quantity of crime-control tools available to the precinct commander.

Using civil remedies to curtail crime, however, rubbed against the grain of the traditional reactive law enforcement approach. Consequently, the civil initiative had some rough sledding. Only demonstrable success, energetic advocates, and an opportune organizational climate could surmount the initial barriers.

The Precinct Commander as Client.   Like many NYPD reforms, the idea of assigning lawyers to the field was not novel. In the 1970s, Commissioner Patrick Murphy, a reformer, lamented the fact that headquarters housed a deputy commissioner for legal matters, yet "out in the field, in the precinct where the real police work was being done, there was nothing."[6] As with most visions, there was a yawning gap between conception and inception. However, by 1991 the CEU had gone beyond Murphy's image of attorneys helping officers make proper arrests. The CEU's lawyers helped precinct commanders to inflict economic damage on criminals. While drug arrests usually just detained some cogs in a criminal enterprise, shutting down a drug location had a much greater impact.

Although theoretically attractive, the practicality of curbing criminal activity through precinct-based civil remedies had to be demonstrated to doubters. Headquarters lawyers typically believed they belonged in their comfortable offices. The city government's legal practice traditionally fell to its law firm, the Corporation Counsel. Criminal prosecutions were forged through long-established collaboration between the district attorney and the NYPD.

Adding civil strategies to the enforcement menu called for new ingredients. For example, nuisance abatement—the crown jewel and most frequently used civil remedy—required detailed evidence of three or more criminal incidents at a particular place. If it was a drug location, evidence of narcotics arrests had to be presented to the court. Documentation of these incidents was drawn from the Narcotics Division's drug operations records. Retrieving this information was extremely difficult and time-consuming prior to Compstat. Robert Messner, managing attorney and, with former Deputy Commissioner of Legal Matters Jeremy Travis, father of the Civil Enforcement Initiative, explained that in the "old pre-Compstat days there was little interest in patterns and history." Narcotics transactions were filed by the particular buy-and-bust operation, not by address. Only laborious examination of log books and records could recoup this information. "Regularizing information sharing was as time-consuming as etching new channels in rock from rushing water," he added. That was just a few years back, but "three years is ancient history. Compstat's scrutiny of trends and patterns has now made it easier for us."

In addition to surmounting archaic record-keeping and information-sharing problems, departmental approval and Corporation Counsel consent were necessary before the initiative could proceed. Change can be costly to organizational players accustomed to established routine. "We were swimming upstream," observed Messner, who with Deputy Commissioner Travis lobbied for the CEU with the department's top command and Corporation Counsel. They were met with mixed reactions. "It made sense to me, but some thought they were crazy. There were many resisters in the department," noted one high-ranking official. As in many success stories, it is difficult now to find people willing to acknowledge their past opposition. Yet resistance was understandable; the lawyers, after all, were civilians, not real cops. What did they know about law enforcement? They meant well, but they were "eggheads."

The advocates, however, had public opinion on their side. Urban disorder spreading throughout the country was provoking a political backlash. Some called the reaction "compassion fatigue"; others named it "disorder fatigue."[7] Courts and legislatures began to support police use of legal remedies and civil injunctions to abate gang activity and to rid public spaces of such nuisances as drinking, littering, drug transactions, and panhandling.[8]

This national mood constituted the backdrop against which the NYPD lawyers were initially permitted limited experimental action. The selection of the NYPD's pilot site was critical. The attorneys preferred high-crime precincts in Brooklyn or Harlem. Fortunately, the lawyers' zeal was tempered with police pragmatism. Police allies, such as the chief of department, David Scott, pointed out that it would be difficult to assess the program's impact in high-crime precincts. Scott recommended the Bronx's 52nd Precinct because of its moderate crime rate and its enlightened, pro–civil enforcement commander, Captain Maurice Collins.

The Bronx became civil enforcement's proving ground. Attorneys and police jointly diagnosed community problems and retrieved information. The street cops' beat books, for example, were surveyed for the identification of areas and bodegas where drugs were sold. In this precomputerized period, the beat books, which listed troublesome conditions, were part of Commissioner Brown's community policing package. The CEU designed Operation Chariot as a response to the drug problem, impounding the cars in which drug dealers and buyers conducted business.

The police and lawyers tailored criminal and civil remedies for other recurring crime and disorder problems. The attorneys used the city's Administrative Code to commence forfeiture actions in New York State Civil Court. The Police Padlock Law was employed to close houses of prostitution. Bar owners near the Bronx's Manhattan College were dissuaded from selling liquor to underage patrons. Operation Soundtrap was devised to address loud car radios. This problem-solving assault on "boom-box" cars was based on a Vehicle and Traffic Law (VTL) provision that makes the loud playing of a car sound system a violation. In cooperation with the Department of Environmental Protection, whose inspectors measured the sound levels of car radios, the NYPD issued summonses to offending drivers and seized their vehicles as evidence. Referring to drivers of boom-box cars, Chief Scott declared, "Blasting their favorite tunes at ear-splitting levels is not only rude, it is against the law and will not be tolerated. If they don't turn off the volume, we'll turn off their ignition."[9] And so the police did just that.

Expanding the Program. The Civil Enforcement Initiative showed striking versatility. The virtual elimination of noted houses of prostitution through the civil Police Padlock Law demonstrated that shutdowns were more effective than traditional raids. Results generated community enthusiasm and spurred praise from the mayor and the Bronx borough president. The Northwest Bronx Community Council clamored for expansion of the program, and in August 1991 three more precincts (the 46th, 48th, and 50th) were added. Once more, civil enforcement lawyers and police proponents forged a crucial alliance.

Inspector Anemone, an active experimenter and strong civil remedies patron, was strategically placed to showcase civil enforcement. Anemone, the future chief of department, was the Bronx divisional commander of two of the three additional civil enforcement precincts in addition to the original 52nd Precinct. When crime declined in his precincts in 1991, he promptly credited the Civil Enforcement Initiative.[10]

An outstanding example of the effectiveness of the CEU was the demise of Jerome Avenue's long-lamented prostitution strip. Jerome Avenue is a major thoroughfare in the northwest section of the Bronx. Repeated arrests of prostitutes had not stemmed the steady supply of replacements and the steady decline in the neighborhood's quality of life. Residents had come to view prostitution as an intractable problem. Attorneys researched the law that allows for the seizure of property used in the furtherance of criminal activity. They designed Operation Losing Proposition to attack the demand side of the problem (the "johns") rather than the supply side (the prostitutes). There was considerable doubt in the NYPD. Would the criminal charges be dismissed in criminal court? Would the civil forfeiture cases against the johns' cars be rejected in court and embarrass the department?

The operation went remarkably smoothly. Female undercover officers posed as street-walking prostitutes and engaged prospective patrons in conversations that resulted in arrests. Civil enforcement attorneys accompanied the police to evaluate the legal basis for the forfeiture of the johns' vehicles. In the first operation, guns and cars were taken from two johns. The courts sustained both the criminal charges and the civil forfeiture cases, and prostitution was greatly reduced. In the words of one cop, "The john may be able to explain a night away from the wife but not the absence of the family car."

The community applauded, and the NYPD followed up. Training and strategies disseminated the procedures of Operation Losing Proposition throughout the department. Eventually, civil enforcement attorneys were not required to be present at each operation.

Success bred further expansion. In July 1992 the CEI spread to the notoriously drug-ridden 34th Precinct in Washington Heights. In a bid to institutionalize civil enforcement and coordinate resources at a cross-precinct level, Commissioner Ray Kelly expanded the initiative in August 1993 to a Queens divisional level that included five precincts. Departmental lawyers and division commanders again joined forces.

Inspector Joseph Raguso, the Queens divisional commander, was the key police activist. Raguso had spent most of his career in middle-class, predominantly white Queens precincts, where problems differed from those plaguing the Bronx and Manhattan's adjacent Washington Heights. But twenty-five years earlier, he had served as a motorcycle cop and sergeant in one of the targeted civil enforcement precincts. The problems back then were remarkably similar to those faced in 1993. Although not the city's highest-crime areas, the precincts were beset with the unruly and seemingly unyielding problem of drag racing on Francis Lewis Boulevard, a major artery, and the hub of a residential area. Accidents (including at least two deaths), loud car radios, disorderly behavior, and other problems triggered resident flight. One irate homeowner, who allegedly placed oil on the boulevard and thereby caused a young racer's death, was acquitted by a jury of his peers.

At the same time, another problem rankled this particular Queens community, known as Bayside. A few blocks from Francis Lewis Boulevard, on Bell Boulevard, more than sixty bars were concentrated in a ten-block stretch. Parking spaces were scarce; patrons parked in homeowners' driveways; crowds congregated; drugs and liquor were peddled; street urination defiled the area; drunken arguments unsettled residents; and the sleepless community was irate.

The police and the attorneys analyzed the problems—they were all intertwined. Bell Boulevard's bars fueled Francis Lewis Boulevard's drunken drag racers and spectators. Upon leaving the bars, patrons headed to Francis Lewis and lined the boulevard. Limit the drinking, CEI advocates came to believe, and you curtail the racing. They started a full-court press on illegal drinking and driving. Law enforcement personnel flooded the bars and bodegas that were selling alcohol to kids. Police and lawyers, along with a State Liquor Authority representative, instructed owners on proper identification procedures and the detection of fake IDs. The message was simple: "Either properly ID patrons or we place uniformed cops in the bar." Police presence in bars was a departure from department policy inaugurated when the Knapp Commission exposed police corruption and urged the reduction of temptations. But Chief of Department Scott decided to take a risk and provide the department with this "hammer."

On the streets, the NYPD enlisted the Department of Transportation (DOT) to place "No Standing" street signs in the residential area adjoining the bars. The bars had also become watering holes for off-duty police; one was shot and killed by a bouncer. Some of the police were part of the problem and not the solution. When illegally parked police cars were sighted, Inspector Raguso had them towed. It was no longer business as usual. On the highways, the police and attorneys set up traffic checks for speeding, DWI, driving with suspended or revoked licenses, and noise violations. They issued tickets and had the DOT seize some cars on the spot. Everything was happening at once. During the first eight weeks, they issued more than 8,000 summonses, arrested over twenty-five individuals, and towed more than 190 vehicles. Over sixty enforcers, including Police Commissioner Kelly and Queens District Attorney Richard Brown, were on the streets at any one time. "It was like a bazaar," recalled one police participant.

After several months of hard police work, the racing had virtually ceased, and bar owners were banning underage drinking. The community was amazed that a problem that had gone unaddressed for a quarter of a century diminished so abruptly.

Queens Councilman Thomas Abel, who had grown up in the area and was closely involved in the quality-of-life crusade, remembered: "It was a dramatic turnaround. If this country was run like that operation, we wouldn't have any problems. I never saw so many agencies work so well together. The NYPD lawyers confiscated these luxury cars as evidence for excessive boombox noise. The young drivers were shocked; so were their parents. There's nothing like losing Daddy's car."

This comprehensive assault on Bayside's problems is a premier example of the NYPD's creative problem solving. When the Queens borough commander reviewed the tactical blueprint, he remarked, "MacArthur did not make this much effort in planning his invasion." One of the officers replied, "His plan was not as good." The campaign was a model of collaboration. The police and attorneys were out on the streets together from 8 P.M. to 4 A.M. "I married Messner," recalled now–Deputy Chief Joseph Raguso. "It was a great comfort to have the attorneys on the scene during these hours. They helped us a great deal by providing the legal sticks when the carrots would not work." Raguso subsequently advanced in the NYPD and, in 1997, relying heavily on civil enforcement, headed a major antidrug initiative in Washington Heights, the city's wholesale drug heartland.[11]

Abating Nuisances. Securing internal permission for expansion is an event; surmounting external resistance is a feat. CEU attorneys not only wanted to extend their market, they also yearned to increase their legal options. The lawyers foresaw great potential in a civil enforcement tool called nuisance abatement. The Nuisance Abatement Law, dating back to 1977, was designed to drive out Times Square massage parlors. However, it is versatile. As the law stipulates, it encompasses many "public nuisances [marked by] the . . . use or alteration of property in flagrant violation of the building code, zoning regulations, health laws, multiple dwelling law, penal laws regulating obscenity, prostitution and related conduct, licensing laws, environmental laws, laws relating to the sale and consumption of alcoholic beverages . . . gambling . . . controlled substances and dangerous drugs . . . stolen property, all of which interfere with the interest of the public in the quality of life and total community environment, the tone of commerce in the city, property values and the public health, safety and welfare." [12]

The Nuisance Abatement Law possesses other possibilities. Prosecutors can commence legal action upon receiving proof of three incidents of illegal activity inside a location. The nuisance abatement actions need not be based on arrests and convictions. The initial application to the New York State Supreme Court seeks a temporary restraining order and temporary closing order. Since these actions do not require advance notice to the opposing party, police benefit from the element of surprise. By contrast, some other remedies, such as the Police Padlock Law, provide advance warning to targets, enabling them to shift operations elsewhere. Nuisance abatement also allows for stiff penalties—up to $1,000 for each day of public nuisance. The fines can serve as a powerful deterrent to landlords who allow their property to be used for illegal activity. Furthermore, while the law requires a hearing to determine if the location should remain closed, most defendants prefer a negotiated settlement, and the vast majority of locations remain closed until the cases are settled. This often takes more than a year.

Although the mayor's Midtown Enforcement Agency and the Corporation Counsel had successfully enforced the ordinance against massage parlors, nuisance abatement had barely touched criminal activity. The Corporation Counsel used the law against criminal activity only thirteen times between 1984 and 1988. To step up the use of nuisance abatement, the NYPD civil enforcement lawyers and their Corporation Counsel counterparts hammered out an agreement permitting the NYPD to pilot nuisance abatement in the Bronx. The Corporation Counsel remained responsible for the rest of the city. During the trial period, NYPD lawyers outpaced the city's attorneys in the volume of cases managed. In addition, a survey revealed thousands of potential cases.

By the middle of 1994, the Corporation Counsel granted the NYPD's civil enforcement lawyers the authority to exercise the abatement remedy throughout the city. It turned out to be a wise decision. Lawyers can tailor nuisance abatement to varied community concerns without alerting criminals in advance. Shifting tactics often catch crooks flat-footed. Targets include drug use and sales locations, houses of prostitution, illegal social clubs, illegal gambling operations, and fencing operations. In 1994, the NYPD filed 214 nuisance abatement cases. Among them were "locations closed including judicial closing orders, evictions by landlords, and abandonment by criminals due to Nuisance Abatement investigations." The number of cases increased to 301 in 1995, 709 in 1996, and 712 in 1997. While the department secured 110 judicial closing orders in 1994, the number increased to 449 in 1996 and 486 in 1997. There were 360 judicial closings in the first seven months of 1998. (This average of 51 closings per month will probably raise the total in 1998 substantially above 500.)[13]

Success was infectious. Additional resources came in the wake of the CEU's territorial and legal expansion. Commissioner Kelly authorized fourteen law clerks to serve the unit's five-member staff. His successor, Commissioner William Bratton, was quick (as was Mayor Giuliani) to recognize civil enforcement's versatility. With the partial support of federal funding, the new administration proudly proclaimed a three-stage approach to increasing the unit staff to forty-five persons by the end of 1994. Adroitly adopting the civil service title of "law clerk" for these new positions, the department could draw from highly competent applicants without relying on time-consuming civil service lists. The NYPD indicated that "in essence, a new law firm will be created, the first of its kind in the country, to provide legal support for community policing strategies."[14]

Mayor Giuliani and Commissioner Bratton prominently featured civil enforcement when they publicly unveiled their strategy for cracking down on quality-of-life offenses. "Reclaiming the Public Spaces of New York" (Strategy Number Five; see Chapter 4 for a discussion of the strategies) granted precinct commanders increased autonomy to tackle prostitution, public urination, aggressive panhandling, public drinking, and other street offenses. To combat prostitution, civil enforcement lawyers (instead of the Public Morals Division or other specialized units) would work with precinct cops on Operation Losing Proposition. Nuisance abatement was extended to fifty-five precincts. "In quality of life," legal bureau head Jeremy Travis noted, "the effective response is a sustained response."[15] The CEU's staff has continued to grow since 1994, and by 1997, it had about sixty-five members. Former Commissioner Murphy's vision of precinct-based attorneys was approaching reality.

Growth and accomplishments generated enthusiasm and recognition. The CEU was honored as a winner of the 1995 Innovations in American Government award from the Ford Foundation and Harvard University's Kennedy School of Government. This prestigious honor funded a video and booklet entitled *The Cutting Edge of Policing: Civil Enforcement for the 21st Century*. In 1997, the Civil Enforcement Unit presented the video and booklet to 16,000 chiefs gathered at the annual conference of the International Association of Chiefs of Police. Civil enforcement was on its way to globalization.

Conclusion

Several reform lessons are embedded in the NYPD civil enforcement journey. Uphill battles can be won, but doing so requires considerable time and important allies, strategically placed. For its first six years, the Civil Enforcement Initiative forged strong links with agile supporters in headquarters and field positions. These people had shared interests in reducing crime and fashioning strategies to solve specific problems. They recognized adaptability as the key to success. Civil enforcement is as effective in the middle-class, tree-lined boulevards of Queens as in the ghetto neighborhoods of the Bronx. Problems may vary, but quality of life is a common concern. The CEI's proponents were greatly aided by Compstat and other post-1994 organizational developments. Compstat converted civil enforcement from a "holding action" to an innovation "taking hold." The combination of civil enforcement and Compstat yielded dramatic crime-reduction results.

Prostitution at the Bronx's seedy, thirty-seven-room Jerome Hotel, for example, had distressed the surrounding neighborhood for several years. Women stood in the entrance, beckoning motorists. Neighbors heard voices over a megaphone, announcing the time remaining in patrons' rooms. Street prostitution and drug activity gravitated to the hotel's parking lot.

Citizens had visited the hotel's owners, but to no avail. The community was up in arms. The local Mount Hope Community Organization demanded action. Since 1994 there had been more than 200 arrests for prostitution-related offenses in the area, 10 undercover investigations, and 45 seizures of johns' cars. Yet the problem remained. It was only when the community organizations, the vice enforcement squad, and the CEU attorneys began to share information and collaborate in nuisance abatement litigation that the hotel was closed down in late 1995.

The community was elated. Brenda Dewingle, who lived near the hotel, said at the time, "I think it's really good because a kids' park is across the street, and you can see everything here. They [the prostitutes] are out here all day long." Sally Jones, who lived on a ridge above the hotel on Davidson Avenue, said, "I'm just so happy, I'm about to get a soda to celebrate. We've been calling the police about the megaphone. Kids can't go to sleep at night because they hear Jane arguing with Mary about this john or that john. Close it down!"[16] More than two years later, at the end of 1997, the hotel was still closed. In addition, the NYPD was negotiating with the owners, offering to recommend forgiveness of their steep fines if they would sell the property to a community nonprofit group.

Compstat statistics and meetings inevitably trigger civil enforcement in precincts with demanding crime problems. The meetings spotlight surges in shootings, and top brass demand reductions. "Every shooting became a big deal after Compstat," recalls a precinct special operations officer, Lieutenant Martin Stein. "The bosses ask questions about what the detectives and others are doing at the crime scene." Imaginative precinct commanders swiftly include carefully crafted civil enforcement in their antiviolence campaigns.

Brooklyn's 81st Precinct, for example, experienced an increase in homicides and shootings in 1995, contrary to the city's downward trend. Although the precinct's overall crime rate dropped, there were nine more homicides in 1995 than in 1994, and ten more shooting incidents.[17] In September 1995 Captain Michael Gabriel became the precinct commander in this predominantly minority community, with just under 62,000 people residing in a 1.7-square-mile area. The neighborhood combines the grand homes and brownstones of Brooklyn's most prominent African Americans with burned-out buildings, vacant lots, and a 30 percent unemployment rate. Gabriel analyzed the portrait of precinct violence and discovered that over a third was drug related. Many drug-selling bodegas were masquerading as legitimate businesses. "We saw a lot of potential there," recalled Gabriel. Lieutenant Stein, Gabriel's special operations officer, remembered his own unfamiliarity with civil enforcement. "Captain Gabriel told us that what is going to win here is nuisance abatement. He taught us." As a former Manhattan narcotics commander, Gabriel had previously used civil enforcement. One of his former officers had remarked that the narcotics detectives had "been hitting the same location for over 14 years" before they shut it down through nuisance abatement.

The attack on drugs and violence, therefore, quickly embraced civil enforcement as part of an inclusive strategy that drew upon civil enforcement attorneys, Street Narcotics and Gun (SNAG) units, anticrime units, intensive detective operations, and federal agents to target drug gangs and quality-of-life offenses. Within four months, the community applauded store shutdowns, though they lamented fewer job opportunities. When two illicit businesses were boarded up, for example, a neighbor reflected on the dilemma: "On the one hand, we need all the businesses and the jobs we get in the neighborhood. But these were not businesses. They were disaster areas, and I'm glad they're shut down."[18]

Illicit store operations fell fast. In 1996, sixteen businesses in the 81st Precinct were closed through court-ordered nuisance abatement. Ralph's Second Hand Dealer, for example, was buying property stolen from neighborhood residences. The precinct responded with three sting operations in which undercover officers fenced stolen property. These tactics enabled the attorneys to close the shop. Residential burglaries fell. An additional twenty stores closed when notified of precinct nuisance abatement proceedings.[19] By the end of 1997, the precinct and lawyers had shut down eighty-one locations. "The public loved it when we got rid of obvious drug spots," notes Gabriel.

Store shutdowns have enormous public appeal. If people do not witness the actual boarding up of the premises, they will see the signs noting "Closed down by the NYPD and court order due to selling of marijuana." Also, without store shutdowns, many "residents believe the police are on the take," observes Lieutenant Stein. "It is the most visible thing we ever did." Visibility also breeds an increase in community calls for greater safety and order.

By the time newly promoted Deputy Inspector Gabriel moved

on to another precinct (two years after he had arrived), statistics dramatically reflected the impact of his tenure. The 81st Precinct had 35 homicides in 1995 but only 15 in 1996, and again 15 in 1997; the 126 shootings in 1995 declined to 58 in 1996 and 38 in 1997. Other crime figures also dropped. These improvements yielded additional benefits. Because there were fewer murders and shootings, detectives had more time for investigations. For example, police made seventeen homicide arrests in connection with 1997's fifteen homicides in the 81st Precinct. The precinct now has the lowest number of citizen drug complaints for commercial establishments among the ten precincts that constitute Brooklyn North. "It all ties together," observes Lieutenant Stein, "and it works."

Even outside observers can see the benefits of combining Compstat and civil enforcement. "Yesterday was final for Club Vinyl," recounted columnist Jack Newfield. He was referring to nuisance abatement proceedings that shut down the club following two shootings, thirty-four drug arrests, and numerous underage drinking summonses within the first five months of 1997. Pending charges include assaults, liquor sales to minors, and sales of LSD and "Special K," a cat tranquilizer popular among teenagers. Newfield reported: "Club Vinyl became notorious after two shootings on hip-hop nights. It even became an issue at the NYPD's weekly COMPSTAT strategic-planning meetings of precinct commanders and NYPD brass."[20]

Civil enforcement also demonstrated unexpected spillover value. In October 1994, for example, an officer assigned to Operation Losing Proposition in the Bronx arrested a man for patronizing a prostitute and seized his van, which was found to contain twenty-seven pipe bombs and other weapons. The accompanying civil enforcement attorney assisted the officer in securing a search warrant for the weapons. Another operation uncovered the much-feared "Midtown Slasher," whose knifing of random victims had terrorized the area through much of 1995.

Before 1994, those who sought new crime-fighting paths did not typify the dominant NYPD organizational culture. The beaten path was more familiar and seemed less costly. Top brass, for example, often discredited precinct commanders with high arrest and overtime rates. Many street cops did not want to make a lot of arrests for fear of getting "jammed up"—spending too much time in court. The lengthy arrest process, moreover, would remove an officer from street patrol, and police visibility was desired by both the department's hierarchy and the neighborhoods.[21] A high rate of arrests could also bring citizens' accusations of corruption or abuse.

Even if New York's crime rates rapidly increased, conventional and scholarly wisdom would more readily blame societal factors than police tactics. Existing practices were therefore favored. COs tried to keep crime as close as possible to current levels and to those of comparable precincts. They also tried to sustain or increase revenue-generating summons activity, which unofficial policy prized more than arrests.[22]

The CEI, on the other hand, grew out of the seeds of reform that were planted before 1994 and later found more fertile soil. The CEI embodies NYPD's shift away from maintaining existing crime levels, and toward decisively dropping them instead. Stability is no longer cherished as the prime objective.

Most important, the CEU shares Compstat's information base and its orientation toward problem solving and future results. In 1994, early in the new Giuliani-Bratton administration, the civil enforcement attorneys presented their agenda to CEI advocate Anemone, who was then the new chief of patrol and a former Bronx divisional commander. The attorneys projected a large map that highlighted precinct problems (such as bodegas selling beer to minors) by color. Key words (such as "nuisance abatement") indicated the appropriate strategy. This was a novel convergence of ideas and approaches—mapping, analyzing problems, and strategizing. Compstat and the CEI are more than compatible and harmonious; they feed off one another, and they need each other to work. In the remarkable October 1994 plan of action, the astute NYPD committee concluded that "this plan is not a menu of options from which items can be selected at random for implementation. Although some recommendations would no doubt produce significant positive results if implemented independently, the plan's real value and potential is in its synergistic effect."[23]

The interplay between Compstat and civil enforcement is crucial. Compstat not only provides the informational support for the CEU; it guides and monitors its effectiveness. When recurrent precinct crime problems arise at Compstat meetings, the inevitable question is "What civil enforcement are you using and what are your results?" What was once "the odd duck," in the words of one of its attorneys, has now become an NYPD workhorse.

Unfortunately, there is an underbelly to reform's success: The more ambitious the transformation, the greater the need for complementary changes. The CEU, despite its innovative orientation, would probably not have made it alone. It needed personal, organizational, and management moorings. Without them, it might have gone the way of other ephemeral NYPD reforms: Here today and gone tomorrow. The CEU needed Compstat and other NYPD changes before it could work effectively. The shutdown of 100 Palmetto Street is a good example. This well-known drug location, after all, spawned crime conditions for over fifteen years, including the first three years of the new Giuliani-Bratton administration. Why did it take so long for the CEU to focus on Palmetto? First, civil enforcement had to be introduced by the NYPD. Second, it had to be extended to Brooklyn. Third, NYPD nuisance abatement had to be sanctioned by the Corporation Counsel. Fourth, the CEU had to be anchored to the Compstat process. But all of this was in place by the middle of 1994, and Palmetto was not shut down until March 1997. Why the delay?

Two ingredients had been missing. The first was a high-ranking Brooklyn police CEI field champion, and the second was an effective field organizational structure. The champion was the Brooklyn North borough commander, Chief Joseph Dunne, and the field development was the new and innovative borough structure (called SATCOM)[24] closely linked to Compstat. Palmetto's closing was spurred by these later advancements. Their origins, development, and wide-ranging ramifications are the subject of the next chapter.

7   **BROOKLYN BOUND**

April 1996
A two-month outbreak of burglaries batters a precinct.

Precinct Commander: "We've set up a burglary team with a sergeant and seventeen police officers to respond to every burglary. They do a canvass of the area and dust for prints. They also work plainclothes. We did not have collars [arrests] at first, but we got some later."

Chief: "I don't see much follow-up on burglary debriefings and talking to these perps. You do it on homicides and shootings, but we don't see it in burglaries. We need information. We need to focus on debriefings. You flooded the area, made collars, but did you do anything about the problem? Where are these guys? Let's treat burglaries like the crimes they are."

A Compstat meeting? Well, sort of. Instead of being held at police headquarters in lower Manhattan, this meeting takes place across the East River at the Mt. Carmel Church in Brooklyn's Williamsburg community. The inquisitors are not headquarters top brass; they are the heads of Brooklyn North—one of the NYPD's eight patrol boroughs. The leaders are questioning the commanders of the ten precincts, ten narcotics units, ten detective squads, and two housing police areas that the Brooklyn North Patrol Borough comprises. The meeting is formally known as a "borough Compstat crime strategy meeting."[1] But everybody in Brooklyn North calls it a "Dunnestat meeting," naming it for Chief Joseph P. Dunne, Brooklyn North's head since February 1996.

Widely respected by the thousands under his command, Dunne has traveled a meteoric career path. His leadership qualities became clear during the tenure of four police commissioners.[2] As commanding officer of Brooklyn North's crime-ridden 75th Precinct, Dunne took advantage of the authority, discretion, and strategies that headquarters had recently dispensed to its precinct commanders. His cops were eager to follow the lead of the new mayor, Rudolph Giuliani, and police commissioner, William Bratton. They had just helped "elect their guy as mayor," Dunne recalled. Morale soared. The cops went after quality-of-life infractions, and Dunne attained dramatic results. Total felony crime numbers dropped from more than 10,000 in 1993 to under 9,000 in 1994 and just over 8,000 in 1995.[3]

Dunne's success and his presentation skills at headquarters Compstat meetings gained him the hierarchy's attention. Within just a few years, he rose from captain to deputy inspector to inspector and then deputy chief in 1995 when he was moved to the Internal Affairs Bureau. When Dunne took over the Brooklyn North command and was elevated to assistant chief, the departing commissioner, William Bratton, was about to be replaced by Howard Safir.

Dunne's questions about precinct burglaries occurred shortly after Brooklyn North was reconstituted as SATCOM (Strategic and Tactical Command) Brooklyn North in April 1996. SATCOM is a unique NYPD venture. As its commander, Dunne has greater authority than any of his seven other borough counterparts. He not only presides over all of SATCOM's patrol forces, but also has unprecedented command of all detectives, drug investigators, and housing police who previously reported to their separate borough and headquarters superiors. "He's the king of police here," remarked a cop under Dunne's command. Antidrug operations, for example, are traditionally run by the Narcotics Division of the Organized Crime Control Bureau, with enforcement and deployment decisions made through its chain of command. Similar functional assignments typically apply to patrol, detective, and housing police operations. SATCOM replaces this functional division of labor with geographically based management. All Brooklyn North police operations are under Chief Dunne, who reports directly to the chief of department. Dunne has become, in essence, a mini–police commissioner for Brooklyn North.

SATCOM is NYPD reform writ large—an amalgam of past accomplishments and weaknesses, promises and pitfalls, reform impulses and bureaucratic caution, managerial vision and political infighting. To understand SATCOM's development, operations, and future is to grasp the complexities, commonalities, and contrasts embedded in the NYPD's reform saga.

SATCOM's Origins

SATCOM's roots are multiple and contradictory. On the one hand, there is a compelling, seemingly natural course in its aims and methods. Its decision to address Brooklyn's drug epidemic made great sense. Many sites like 100 Palmetto Street underpinned the borough's bruised reputation.

Brooklyn North, with a population of over 800,000, about 12 percent of New York City's total, produced more than a quarter of the city's 1995 drug complaints, 27 percent of its shooting victims, 20 percent of citywide murders, and 19 percent of its robberies. Six of Brooklyn North's ten precincts were high drug-trafficking areas, two were moderate and only two were desig-

nated low-incident areas. Brooklyn neighborhoods such as Bushwick, Bedford-Stuyvesant, Williamsburg, Fort Green, Brownsville, and East New York abounded in narcotics-driven crime
and violence. One observer described these areas as places where
"crime is as common as the wash that hangs on clotheslines in
the backyards of the neighborhoods."[4]

There should be no surprise, therefore, that great fanfare and
numerous briefings accompanied SATCOM's April 1996 unveiling. Mayor Giuliani pronounced its goals: to "come as close as
we can come to crushing drug trafficking and the drug business" in Brooklyn North.[5] At a Compstat meeting two days earlier, outgoing Deputy Commissioner Jack Maple insisted that
SATCOM would become the "greatest narcotics operation in the
history of the country only if we improve our coordination level,
attention to detail, and discipline." Maple declared that the attack on street-level, indoor drug dealing and its organizational
backers would reduce the city's felony crimes by over 20 percent.
If the goals make sense, why not marshal all NYPD resources in
a coordinated borough effort? The department, after all, was constantly touting its transfer of headquarters authority and decision making to lower command tiers.[6]

On another level, however, the SATCOM move was far from
natural; it was a risky, almost revolutionary, undertaking. Crime
had dropped during the first two years of the new Giuliani-
Bratton administration. Brooklyn North's felony rate had plunged
an impressive 28 percent. Even Brownsville's notorious 73rd Precinct flattened its homicide total from 74 in 1993 to 47 in 1994
and 28 in 1995. The 75th Precinct in East New York dropped
from 126 homicides in 1993 (the highest in the city) to 87 in 1994
and 44 in 1995. This 65 percent two-year drop in the 75th precinct was the largest among all the city's precincts. Why experiment now? Would not combating drugs with an entirely new organizational setup be tampering with success? Would this new
Brooklyn North geographically based management weaken the

NYPD's citywide antidrug command structure? Drug dealers are not confined by boundary lines; they travel between Brooklyn and Manhattan. This was of great concern to the Organized Crime Control Bureau and its Narcotics Division, NYPD's antidrug enforcers. Furthermore, why replace Brooklyn North's current commander with a precinct commander who, although effective, had no borough-level experience?

The wisdom of the SATCOM decision was not self-evident. The department's risky venture sat at the confluence of many tributaries: reengineering and departmental politics, drugs and crime, and Compstat.

Reengineering and Departmental Politics.   The reengineering committees (see Chapter 4) set the tone for many departmental developments. One such committee's July 1994 report, comparing geographically based with functional organizations, supplied the premises for the SATCOM experiment. The police commissioner's charge to the committee was to "create the most effective and efficient organizational structure to dramatically reduce crime . . . by putting resources, responsibility, and authority at the lowest feasible levels of the organization. This must apply especially to precinct commanders." The committee proposed a "major rebuilding," acknowledging that "change in this Department, one of the largest and probably most tradition-bound police departments in the world, has come historically very slowly."[7] Given the commissioner's mandate, the question was not whether but to what extent resources, authority, and responsibility would be thrust down to the borough and precinct levels. The twenty-three-member committee included virtually all the top brass and some lower-ranking officers.[8] In committee debate, two groups of active participants with sharply contrasting views were pitted against each other. The first group, primarily those elevated by and more closely linked to Commissioner Bratton, pressed for far-reaching geographic decentralization.[9]

They favored transferring supervision of detective and narcotics operations from headquarters to borough or precinct levels.

Not surprisingly, the committee members more closely allied with headquarters bureaus contested restrictions on their authority. They distrusted diminished crime-fighting flexibility, such as the ability to pursue a serial killer stalking victims in several boroughs,[10] and they favored the conventional, functional mode of management. They viewed geographic decentralization as a power grab masquerading as innovative management. "There was a lot of jockeying and lobbying going on," recalled one participant. "The stakes were high."

Proposals to push narcotics and detective operations to lower levels did not emerge from the committee; this transfer had to wait for SATCOM, which was created two years later. Nevertheless, the committee's endorsement of significant shifts in authority prepared the way. The department quickly adopted committee proposals to grant precinct commanders authority to deploy their anticrime units in decoy operations, a function previously reserved for the citywide street-crime unit. Precinct personnel were now permitted to execute felony arrest warrants and to act as plainclothes officers for public morals enforcement. This was a departure from the long-standing prohibition against precinct-level enforcement of offenses traditionally associated with police corruption. The NYPD also followed the report's recommendation to remove restrictions on the total number of personnel that precinct commanders could assign to precinct specialty units.

The report sharply criticized multilayered NYPD reporting practices as impediments to speedy and effective enforcement and urged turf-based deployment. For example, the reengineering committee recommended transferring Street Narcotics and Gun (SNAG) units and the Public Morals Division (later the Vice Enforcement Squad) from the Narcotics Division to the boroughs and also moving all detective operations from headquarters to the boroughs. This arrangement, the committee said, would provide the patrol boroughs and the precincts with "high visibility and immediate impact on quality-of-life issues that frequently are the precinct commanders' primary problems."[11] SATCOM is a direct descendant of geographic management.

Drugs and Crime. Drugs and attendant street disorder had commanded NYPD's center stage since Giuliani's 1993 mayoral campaign (see Chapter 4). One of the new administration's strategies targeted drugs and crime. Drugs were said to be the city's "main engine of crime. People rob and steal to keep using drugs, and people kill and maim to keep selling drugs."[12] More than 25 percent of homicides were directly tied to drugs; over three-quarters of robbery suspects testified positive for drugs; and over 80 percent of weapons-charge suspects and burglary suspects tested positive. The NYPD strategy called for an aggressive campaign against open-air drug markets, with emphasis on the detection, arrest, and prosecution of narcotics dealers. In a candid self-appraisal of its previous enforcement tactics, the department found that while it had "reclaimed" certain areas of the city from drug dealers, "it had inadequate resources, insufficiently coordinated efforts, and too-limited participation by Patrol Services personnel to be able to hold these areas long enough for neighborhoods to help reestablish themselves as drug-free."[13] The department declared a "No Tolerance" policy for drug dealers and purchasers through tactical refocusing of police personnel and resources. Previously, uniformed patrol officers, who were obviously in an ideal position to observe narcotics operations, were discouraged from making street-level drug arrests. Previous administrations were "concerned that the temptations of the lucre of narcotics trafficking would be too great."[14]

The new strategy proposed a straightforward solution—allow patrol personnel to act against narcotics activity that they witness. Precinct commanders could now permit their street narcotics units to work in plainclothes and target specific locations. They would be backed with additional manpower, more timely and accurate information, round-the-clock operations, and more sophisticated training. The strategy provided that when SNAG units uncovered criminal activity seemingly unrelated to narcotics (such as auto theft, prostitution, or gambling), details of the cases would be referred to the patrol and the appropriate investigative division of the Organized Crime Control Bureau. In this way, the department would seek to keep known instances of criminal activity from falling through the cracks due to overspecialization. Policies were revised to strengthen coordination and widen information sharing among patrol, narcotics, detective, and civil enforcement units. This strategy, as we shall see, blossomed in the SATCOM environment.

The department wasted little time in developing a massive and ambitious antidrug plan. Operation Juggernaut aimed for "total and complete disruption of drug trafficking and attendant crime" through a five-borough, phased infusion of 3,500 additional narcotics officers. Formulated in the fall of 1994, Juggernaut was scheduled for a January 1995 launch in Queens; its final phase was planned for Brooklyn and Staten Island in July 1996. Commissioner Bratton claimed, however, that Mayor Giuliani's initial ardor for the plan was cooled by a December 1994 *Daily News* headline calling it "Bratton's Juggernaut."[15] With the mayor no longer aboard, Operation Juggernaut had a brief shelf life. Yet SATCOM and subsequent drug initiatives revived Juggernaut's proposed orchestration of round-the-clock narcotics operations. "Juggernaut served as a template for us," recalled SATCOM's Chief Joseph Dunne.[16]

Compstat and SATCOM.   SATCOM is partially a Compstat creation. While reengineering and drug strategies shaped SATCOM's contours, internal NYPD maneuvering and the Compstat unit designed its blueprint. The Compstat office is affiliated with the same chief of department, Louis Anemone, who was a forceful advocate for geography-based policing when he was a member of the reengineering committee.

SATCOM was, in part, a response to a January 1996 effort to quash drug gangs and drug distribution stores in three Lower East Side Manhattan precincts.[17] This operation reported to the Narcotics Division of Chief Martin O'Boyle's Organized Crime Control Bureau. The division's sixty additional narcotics officers were crucial to this antidrug activity. Chief Anemone and Deputy Commissioner Maple, however, argued that even more anti-crime "bang for the buck" could be racked up in Brooklyn North than in Manhattan. Their proposal was a captivating composite of antidrug strategies, geography-based management, and internal political maneuvers. The more the department based its organization on borough geography, the more power accrued to the chief of department. Narcotics investigators, street patrol, detectives, and housing police—who normally reported up the ladder to their bureau chiefs at headquarters—were now accountable to SATCOM's Chief Dunne, who reported directly to Chief of Department Anemone.

At SATCOM's opening meeting, Chief Anemone described SATCOM as a "management laboratory, a smarter way of doing business. This signature piece will be the NYPD's boldest attack on narcotics." If this laboratory was extended to all boroughs, it would sap the potency of headquarters bureau chiefs, and the chief of department would be even more powerful.

SATCOM's design illustrates the informal side of Compstat. The latter is far more than an information book and crime strategy meeting. Its organizational dynamics tell an important story. As noted earlier, the handful of individuals reporting to the chief of patrol in 1994 and then, beginning in 1995, to the chief of department (when he was promoted) possess vast formal authority and informal influence.[18] Thus, it was no surprise that the chief of department's office fashioned SATCOM. "Anemone has made the chief's office far more powerful," one dynamic field commander commented approvingly. "Our job would be radically different without him. He is the most knowledgeable and motivated. Compstat meetings without him are Compstat Lite." Brooklyn North's configuration could not have arisen elsewhere. On being ordered to report directly to SATCOM, the organized crime control, detective, patrol, and housing field units lost a great deal of their autonomy.

How would this experiment fare? SATCOM was conceived during the tenure of one police commissioner, but implemented under the leadership of his successor. An April 9, 1996, SATCOM meeting occurred eight days after the program kickoff and six days before Bratton left office. The commissioner's fleeting presence at this meeting was one of his last police appearances. It was a bittersweet interlude. Bratton briefly bid adieu to the group, observing how SATCOM was critical to the evolution of the department's geographic decentralization. "This is something that has been in the works for two years," he said. "You have my sincere appreciation. I wish you every success. I envy you the opportunity to participate in this work. This will be the professional envy of the world."

On April 15, 1996, fourteen days after SATCOM's unveiling, Howard Safir was sworn in as New York City's thirty-ninth police commissioner. Safir immediately endorsed SATCOM: "Our Anti-Drug Initiative in Brooklyn North is the largest sustained attack on entrenched drug dealing in the history of this country. It is the most important strategic move we can make against crime." [19] Nevertheless, questions remained. What kind of support would SATCOM receive from the new commissioner, the chief of department, and Compstat? Would opponents at headquarters cramp its effectiveness? How would its crime-fighting fortunes compare to other patrol boroughs' conquests? How would the department react? How long would this geography-based organization remain in place? Would the SATCOM arrangement be extended to other boroughs? How would the key SATCOM players fare in their careers? These inquiries reveal much about the NYPD's changing dance partners—reform, resistance, and reconfiguration.

SATCOM Success

SATCOM got off to a running start. Between January 1996 and SATCOM'S official April 1 debut, Dunne was affiliated with the chief of department's office. In this brief period, Dunne, along with Compstat and other personnel, did the following:

- identified SATCOM command staff
- selected, processed, trained, and certified hundreds of additional narcotics officers to supplement the Brooklyn North contingent
- located suitable facilities and sites for housing these officers
- targeted over 250 Brooklyn North drug sites
- worked with the Brooklyn district attorney's office to speed up the processing of narcotics arrests and to increase the number of attorneys, computers, and courtrooms
- made numerous briefings to headquarters brass and politicians.

"It was a hectic period," recalled Deputy Inspector Ed Young, who headed Chief Anemone's Quality Control Section, a policy analysis unit. Young took the staff lead in logistical planning for SATCOM. His extensive knowledge of the NYPD's bureaucratic labyrinth was critical. Young helped to rapidly transform the initial SATCOM narcotics initiative model into an operational unit. "We had to work the building big time," Young recalled.

That meant coordinating the following headquarters overhead commands:

- Administrative Services Division (for space and construction)
- Budget Unit (for funding)
- Narcotics Division (for "buy money," cars, radios, and other equipment)
- Personnel Bureau (for transferring personnel into SATCOM)
- Management Information Systems (for computers)
- Telephone Control Unit (for phones).

Dunne and company worked seven days a week to meet their deadline.

SATCOM catapulted into action. Its first week of operation saw a more than 15 percent drop in crime compared to the same period a year earlier. During its first three weeks, there was a 98.2 percent increase in arrests, accomplished with a 61 percent increase in personnel. In addition, sixty-one search warrants were executed, compared with sixteen for the same period the previous year, representing a 281 percent increase. These searches yielded evidence of criminal activity that was crucial to the later nuisance abatement closings of 100 Palmetto Street and other drug havens. Six weeks into operations, Dunne told a SATCOM meeting that they had achieved a 16 percent decline in crime compared to the previous year. "Let's double the citywide rate of 10 percent," he exhorted them.

In its first four months, SATCOM recorded 5,785 narcotics and other arrests, in contrast with 1,982 for the same period in 1995.[20] The narcotics operation jolted criminals. As SATCOM shifted into high gear in the summer of 1996, its results were even more impressive. Both July and August had weekly crime drops of more than 20 percent compared to 1995. During the week of August 19–25, for example, felony crime plunged more than 30 percent compared to the same week in 1995, and shooting incidents plummeted more than 58 percent.

By summer's end, SATCOM had hit the big time. During its first five months, murder declined 25 percent, rape 2 percent, robbery 24 percent, felony assault 17 percent, burglary 27 percent, grand larceny 21 percent, auto theft 35 percent, and shooting victims 33 percent. These percentages translated into 37 fewer murders, 6 fewer rapes, 1,597 fewer robberies, 711 fewer assaults, 1,570 fewer burglaries, 694 fewer grand larcenies, 1,276 fewer auto thefts, and 223 fewer people shot. Compared to the same period a year before, there were 5,738 fewer victims of major crimes in Brooklyn North. When Brooklyn North's pre-SATCOM period (January 1 to March 31) was included in calculations, the command's almost 19 percent decline exceeded the citywide decline of less than 14 percent for this January to August 1996 period. SATCOM surpassed its 1996 goal with an annual decline in crime of almost 20 percent. This drop not only exceeded the citywide 1996 decline of 13.67 percent but also outstripped each of the other seven patrol boroughs. Flexible policing and free-flowing information had shown remarkable success.

Searching SATCOM.   SATCOM's geographically fused operations were designed to combat the "silo syndrome," in which separate units act independently. The borough wanted to avoid repetition of Deputy Commissioner for Operations Edward Norris's Compstat grilling of a commander about why drug-related crime was increasing in his precinct. "I don't have much drug intelligence. My precinct doesn't have an SNEU [Street Narcotics Enforcement Unit]," replied the commanding officer. Norris responded: "Then why aren't you getting information from borough narcotics? And why is the borough not providing this to the precinct?" Absence of information is a venial sin; failure to acquire information is the road to purgatory.

Borough Blockages.   SATCOM fast-forwarded NYPD's advances in gathering information. The 1994 reengineering strategies (see Chapter 4) deplored information gaps that impeded investigations and enforcement. Officers making juvenile arrests, for example, had no direct access to the city's Juvenile Justice Information Service (JJIS), the computerized system for tracking all family court criminal matters. Therefore, they had difficulty determining whether youthful suspects had prior court records, outstanding warrants, or involvement in other active cases. The result was that dangerous youths went free. The new strategy mandated data inputting and cross-referencing of all juvenile reports, truancy youth referrals, and gang intelligence "in a format that can first be used by precinct personnel and ultimately be interfaced with the JJIS."[21]

The strategies also pressed for expansion of existing databases, such as NITRO (Narcotics Investigative Tracking of Recidivist Offenders), designed to keep tabs on career felony drug offenders. The NYPD arduously collected intelligence on hundreds of the city's known drug locations and small-time dealers. This database was designed to encourage detective, patrol, and other units to collect and retrieve narcotics information previously unavailable or difficult to obtain at the precinct level.[22] Today, it is a rare Dunnestat meeting at which there are no references to databases, such as the comment "The perp has four NITROs."

SATCOM expanded. It crafted a unit to coordinate investigative and crime-strategy intelligence gathering and tracking. This Criminal Intelligence Coordination Unit consolidated several Brooklyn North intelligence units previously scattered around the borough. The unit is located in SATCOM's headquarters building. Its leader, Deputy Inspector Ed Young, came from the chief of department's office, where he had helped transform SATCOM's plan into an operational reality. "We unlock the silos with information," he said. The unit coordinates borough gang enforcement and intelligence debriefing reports. It notifies precincts of hot spot clusters and crime patterns and trends. Its PIM (Pattern Identification Module) "informationals," or crime pattern bulletins (see Chapter 5), are based on analyses of crime reports. For example, within six weeks there had been seven robberies of delivery men in SATCOM'S 79th and 81st Precincts, which adjoin each other. A PIM informational detailed the incidents and reported that armed robbers committed six of the crimes during the day tour. Complainants were making deliveries in all cases. In two of them, oil was being delivered; two other incidents involved a bodega delivery. The PIM also described the suspects' physical charactcristics. Weeks later, uniformed officers in their patrol car responded to a radio call for a robbery in progress. The precinct robbery squad already had staked out this robbery-prone area. The squad responded when patrol described the suspect's camouflage jacket, which jibed with the description in the informational. The squad questioned the suspect, who acknowledged his involvement in the other robberies and also gave up his two accomplices. "The PIM helped us," a robbery squad member recalled. "It made us alert to the pattern. It gave us focus."

In addition, the Criminal Intelligence Coordination Unit installed a ceiling for each crime for each of SATCOM's ten precincts. When this threshold is exceeded, the unit explores related crime patterns and trends in other precincts. Thus, when auto crime surged in three precincts, the unit requested precinct plans to combat and monitor these crimes. Captain Thomas Gangone of SATCOM's 94th Precinct crafted a comprehensive, five-page plan to reduce auto theft, centering on the NYPD's prominently displayed four-part Compstat "mantra."[23]

The first principle, "accurate and timely intelligence," encompassed tactics such as these:

- cooperating with outside agencies (the marshals' and sheriffs' offices and the Department of Sanitation) on recovery locations of abandoned vehicles

- daily grand larceny auto (GLA) analysis and information sharing with adjoining precincts (since many vehicles stolen from the 94th Precinct are recovered in the 104th Precinct)
- posting pictures of GLA parolees and individuals recently arrested for GLA, including those who live, or were arrested, in the 94th Precinct
- posting locations of suspected chop shops (illegal car dismantling operations).

The second Compstat precept, "rapid deployment," suggested the following:

- increasing vehicle safety checkpoints and distributing flyers publicizing these operations
- ensuring that fingerprint officers examine recovered vehicles
- rigorous observation of suspected chop shops
- supporting the auto crime and other NYPD units.

The third tenet, "effective tactics," discussed the following:

- joint enforcement, with the Civil Enforcement Unit, of the legal and licensing requirements for automobile repair businesses, some of which are fronts for organized auto crime
- joint checkpoints with other precincts
- coordination with Brooklyn North Narcotics when GLA clusters abut narcotics locations.

"Relentless follow-up and assessment," the fourth commandment, entailed these measures:

- tracking all GLA arrestees until final case disposition to ensure they are present or a warrant is issued

- identifying, computerizing data on, and tracking recidivist auto thieves
- visiting recent GLA parolees to gain their assistance as CIs (confidential informants)
- linking with the Division of Parole and Department of Corrections computer systems.

In addition to these four Compstat yardsticks, Captain Gangone added a fifth category, "public awareness." Illustrative items included crime prevention lectures for the public, newspaper articles, store visits, and literature alerts on upcoming operations.

Increased precinct vehicle checkpoints, greater attention to auto chop shops and parolees, and public involvement yielded dramatic results. Interagency teamwork also recovered autos abandoned for insurance money. Intense SATCOM operations reversed the rising tide of car thefts. In three months, the multipronged approach was able to halt the 113 percent increase of the previous two months and drop auto theft an additional 23 percent.

Spikes in GLA and other crimes continually command Compstat and Dunnestat attention. Precinct problems are scrutinized, operational assumptions are challenged, tactics are queried, options are proposed, and participants are admonished and exhorted.

The wave of precinct auto crimes swept Compstat and Dunnestat for months. Here are examples of how those meetings addressed the problem.

COMPSTAT MEETING: Chief Anemone to precinct commander: "What's going on here? Are you working with the Brooklyn Auto Larceny Task Force, the Auto Crime Division? Where are the autos being recovered? What is the pattern here? Have you checked chop shops for licenses? Have you targeted their licenses? Have any outside agencies given out summonses? Let's move on this."

DUNNESTAT MEETING: Chief Dunne to precinct commander: "How well are we debriefing these people who claim
their cars have been stolen? We need information. Are you using the MARCH [Multi-Agency Response to Community Hot-
spots[24]] program? Where are you doing checkpoints? What are
you doing about minicheckpoints? Are they directed checkpoints? Who directs them? If we get a handle on GLAs in the 73
and 75 [precincts], it will have a big impact." Inspector William
Allee (SATCOM's narcotics head) to precinct commander: "If
you need undercovers for stings, call us."

Information flows through the Compstat-Dunnestat-precinct
nexus. SATCOM prods this flow. The face-to-face encounters
among detectives and patrol, narcotics, housing, and transit officers help scale the barricades. According to Lieutenant Joseph
Cardinale, head of Brooklyn's robbery squad, the borough meetings "enable the left hand to let the right hand know what's
being done. Now the detective squads and precincts have much
greater coordination. Dunne does it right." Detectives are frequently queried about how thoroughly they debrief arrestees and
search for accomplices. Follow-up investigations are scrutinized,
and officers are asked whether they use quality-of-life offenses to
elicit new information. Similarly, investigators are probed about
the type and number of their confidential informants. There is
no reluctance to make unit comparisons and render judgments,
and laggard units are prodded.

Broadway Bound.   Dunnestats demand and disseminate crime
information. A journalist from Ireland reported home on a
Dunnestat meeting: "We're in a synagogue because the Brooklyn police were never expected to have big meetings like this—
with more than 60 officers and observers—and had nowhere else
to hold it. So the local Jewish leaders have agreed to allow the
police to discuss robberies, rapes, and killings in their place of
worship."[25]

A May 1996 meeting opens when Chief Dunne introduces a representative from the city's Parks Department. "We have to plan for security at the city's pools for the summer," notes Dunne. "We need to make sure we are all on the same page for possible outbreaks of violence." SATCOM's Sergeant Paul Scott addresses the meeting after the parks representative's discussion of summer pool security plans. Scott, a key member of the Intelligence Unit, has just returned from a headquarters Compstat meeting. He reports the major topics: auto crime techniques, Queens car-checkpoint detour techniques ("Chief Anemone was impressed"), the centralized operations and training of Staten Island print dusters, and pursuing credit card fraud all the way to the top with credit card companies. "We have to be prepared for these issues," Scott reminds the group.

The meeting shifts to precinct concerns. The 75th Precinct (which Dunne once commanded) dropped in overall crime but soared in burglaries during the past two weeks. The precinct commander, Deputy Inspector Edward Mezzadri, the heads of his detective and narcotics units, and other senior officers discuss the situation and are questioned. Distinct clusters of precinct burglaries are displayed on a map projected on a screen. "What's going on there?" asks Dunne. "What are you doing? Are you doing any stings?" The detective commander reports that his unit just completed a sting that yielded $6,000 worth of stolen jewelry. Dunne is unimpressed: "Has the jewelry been linked to these burglaries?" The detective responds, "No, but we're working on that."

Deputy Inspector Mezzadri comes forward. "We have a new focus," he says. "We set up a burglary unit which also tracks burglary parolees who have come home." But SATCOM records show no arrests of sellers of stolen goods. "Where are the fencing operations and fencing arrests for this year?" Dunne asks. "We're getting into six months of the year, and I want to see something more proactive." Dunne's executive officer, Inspector Joseph Esposito, follows up: "Let's see your drug arrests on top of the burglaries." The map shows both converging in the same precinct cluster. Esposito queries the narcotics commander about his debriefings of arrestees: "We need information. I know you want your narcotics collars, but we want to know everything that's going on."

Another precinct commander is grilled. Shooting incidents have soared in the last thirty days. The previous Dunnestat directed rooftop operations to seize youths testing their handguns. The police can later match rooftop ballistic evidence with crime scene bullets. Dunne asks, "Where is the rooftop plan? What have you done?" The precinct commander is flustered: "Uh, I sent a memo on that to . . ." Dunne interrupts. "Don't ever say you addressed a problem with a memo," he barks. "That doesn't go here or at Compstat."

By generating, circulating, and refining information, Dunnestats are rehearsal sessions—out-of-town tryouts for the "real Compstat" shows. The scripts range from technicalities to major issues. Accuracy of crime complaint reports is critical. Has a precinct downgraded a burglary, which entails a break-in, to the lesser charge of grand larceny? Has a maid's theft of a hotel guest's scarf been upgraded from a grand larceny to a burglary, enabling the politically connected hotel owner to collect insurance? Has a serious felony assault been downgraded to a lesser misdemeanor assault, which is then omitted from the seven major crimes that are tracked by Compstat? One precinct commander reports that every "61" (crime complaint report) is reviewed by a specialist for accuracy. "This is not enough," Dunne interjects. "You need to initial it. Otherwise, Chief Anemone and Compstat will assume you have not read it." On another occasion, a precinct commander begins reporting on a program that was successful in reducing juvenile robberies. "Good example," Dunne interrupts. "Let's save that for Friday [Compstat meeting]."

Violent crime eclipses all issues. In 1995, the housing police and transit police were folded into the NYPD. Merger opponents feared that the additional 6,000 NYPD officers would be used to combat crime in the streets rather than in public housing, ignoring its substantial minority population.[26] Nevertheless, public housing crime declined for almost a year. In the spring of 1996, however, crime jumped in the 73rd Precinct. That one-square-mile area contains the city's largest concentration of public housing, the massive, seventy-seven-building Brownsville complex, where 16,000 residents live within twenty-one blocks. Residents and the media denounced the burglaries (up 20 percent), robberies, shootings, and assaults besieging Brownsville.

To address the Brownsville crime wave, SATCOM and the 73rd Precinct assembled Operation 73—a multipronged attack that drew on proven tactics and inventive, coordinated strategies. Patrol, housing, and narcotics officers joined in perimeter foot and car patrols outside the buildings and conducted "vertical patrols" inside the buildings' staircases. Mounted patrols displayed a police presence, and the NYPD aviation unit surveyed rooftops for stockpiles of bottles and bricks. "Everything was going on at once," recalled a patrol officer who participated in Operation 73. Sergeant John Conicello, head of the Brooklyn Warrant Squad, provided additional support. "We knew the precinct needed help in proactive quality-of-life and warrant enforcement," he observed. Precinct commander Nash coordinated the effort, with SATCOM approval and encouragement. Added Captain Guy R. Sino, head of the Brownsville housing police unit, "Gordon and I meet regularly, a kind of mini-Compstat. We have a job to do, and we do it."

Nash and his executive officer, newly appointed and promoted Captain Ronald Shindel—Operation 73's key architect—installed a temporary command post in the complex to house the police and keep at hand the information they needed. "We were confident that the bulk of the precinct's criminals either resided in or had associates who lived in the complex," Shindel explained. Police showed photo files of burglars to victims of these localized crimes. In addition, transit captains Ruldoph Rognon and James Reilly helped forge STRAP (Street Robbery Abatement Program), in which transit and patrol teams jointly policed troubled subway stops adjoining the Brownsville complex. "We intensified existing tactics and combined precinct and SATCOM resources," explained Nash. "More amazingly, we communicated well with the narcotics units. They would let us know if they were investigating a case in the area so we would withdraw. On the other hand, if they wanted us to do enforcement in the area so they could do debriefings, they would let us know. Unlike in some boroughs, we [SATCOM precincts] do not compete with narcotics [units]."

Operation 73 ran from the end of April to the end of November 1996. It was SATCOM at its best—rapid and coordinated campaigns fueled by free-flowing information. Like computer-screen icons, police units were quickly clicked on and shifted when necessary. Just under 500 felony and more than 900 misdemeanor arrests were made during Operation 73's seven months. Thirty of these arrests were for major index crimes, while several hundred were for drugs and twenty-eight were for guns. The record was nothing short of spectacular: The operation was primarily responsible for the precinct's more than 25 percent across-the-board crime plunge during that period.[27]

The statistics translated into effusive approval by housing project residents. One resident observed, "Before, shootings were every day, every night. You kind of had to duck and run. Now I don't hear shooting in months." Another resident, Thomas Mann, said, "You feel safer walking the streets. Before you didn't hardly see any cops. Now you see them walking around, you feel much safer." Standing outside her building, Sheila Taylor noted: "When you call, cops come more rapidly. If there are drug dealers in the building and cops know where they are, they come and get them." The president of the 73rd Precinct Community Council declared: "Crime has been reduced a whopping amount. My seniors are happy that robbery, burglary, and muggings are down. These are the quality-of-life things people are worried about."[28]

Dunnestat reviewed Operation 73's stellar performance. After listening to precinct commander Nash's Dunnestat presentation, Chief Dunne instructed him to provide slides of the Brownsville area for the upcoming Compstat meeting. Although there is a general rotational schedule for precinct Compstat appearances, precincts may be called back the following week if their crime is still surging. Brownsville's crime had subjected the 73rd precinct to a recall. But Chief Anemone praised Nash at the meeting: "We had you on recall. In the previous week there was a 30 percent increase, and now this week there is a 28 percent decline, so there's a total swing of 58 percent. Good work."

Portable Police. SATCOM's "good work" results from its ability to share information and organize maneuvers. These strengths are not unique to Brooklyn North; many NYPD reforms stem from such advances. What makes SATCOM distinctive is its organizational and managerial capacity to react quickly. A Friday night social club shooting, for example, would typically be reported to the precinct's commanding officer on a Monday. The CO's request for help would travel a tortuous route, from the borough commander through the hierarchy to the chief of patrol. The chief would then pass the request to the chief of department, who, if he approved, would transfer the request to the chief of the Organized Crime Control Bureau, who generally consults with his Narcotics and Vice Enforcement Divisions.[29] If the request was denied, that response would be conveyed back through the chief of department and the chief of patrol, finally reaching the CO, the precinct commander. In the best of circumstances, the process could take weeks, even if the request was accepted. By that time, the problem might have worsened or disappeared. The SATCOM method, by contrast, is direct. The CO would call Dunne, who, if he agreed, would direct the SATCOM Narcotics Unit to do a "buy and bust" to secure witness information. Dunne would also direct SATCOM's Vice Squad to obtain evidence to close the club down.

SATCOM also batters jurisdictional barriers by blurring distinctions. "We're not patrol, we're not the squad (detectives), and we're not the narcs—we're the police. We're generalists; we're not just specialists," Dunne declares. "If you're a cop and you work for me and you're available, you are now a resource, and we will deploy you in a manner that suits our needs." While SATCOM narcotics investigators are assigned to particular precincts around the clock, they, like everybody else, have downtime. Therefore, they regularly help patrol issue summonses for quality-of-life infractions when narcotics enforcement is unnecessary or ineffective. Narcotics investigators issued over 2,700 quality-of-life summonses during SATCOM's first six months, compared with fewer than 100 for the same period the previous year. In addition, investigators are no longer the only officers who execute search warrants. All units, including patrol, are now enlisted. This is important because court-ordered search warrants enable police to seize large cash and drug supplies. Warrants may also turn up dealers' business records. This evidence can yield indispensable information and bolster prosecution. More than 800 search warrants were executed in SATCOM's first sixteen months.

Five months into its operations, SATCOM made further inroads into jurisdictional partitions when it folded narcotics officers, vice officers, and detectives into one investigative unit. Coordinated field homicide and other serious crime investigations stretched the geographic principle. This "streamlined command gives us great mobility," asserted Inspector William Taylor, SATCOM's commanding officer of Detective/Narcotics Operations. "Our units are dedicated to specific precincts, but they are fluid and collapsible. They are able to go wherever they are needed." This arrangement enables narcotics officers and detectives to conduct joint investigations of shooting incidents where drugs are a factor, as they are in 80 percent of SATCOM shootings. After a shooting like those that occurred at 100 Palmetto Street, for example, narcotics officers appear with their intelligence books, called "set books." The books contain photographs of people who frequently hang out in the area. Undercover police seek to obtain investigative leads. "We work to get information early on," Taylor asserts.

Having multiple units under one command smoothes relationships between such outside groups as the Drug Enforcement Agency; Customs Service; Bureau of Alcohol, Tobacco, and Firearms; FBI; Secret Service; Marshals Service; federal and state parole and probation departments; and the district attorney's office. Some joint operations target fugitives wanted for criminal acts—often parole offenders and defendants who failed to appear at criminal court. Working with those agencies, SATCOM apprehended more than 8,000 fugitives in its first sixteen months. Robert N. Kaye, Brooklyn's deputy district attorney (who works closely with Brooklyn police), lauded the approach: "SATCOM works. SATCOM found the enemy and it is us. When narcotics, patrol, and detectives all come under one jurisdiction, there is no way to throw the ball elsewhere."

SATCOM's structure also works well for NYPD Deputy Managing Attorney Johnathan David, head of the Brooklyn and Staten Island staff of the Civil Enforcement Unit (CEU). Initially, however, the attorneys had to overcome soaring caseloads and discordant police goals. "When SATCOM took over Brooklyn North," explains David, "we were very busy. The borough leaned heavily on nuisance abatement's antidrug capacity, and our caseload increased three or four times." Civil enforcement attorneys do not regulate the flow of nuisance abatement cases; they must react to precinct demand. But NYPD patrol and narcotics cops often do not share similar goals. Precinct patrol is more responsive to chronic community complaints about drug locations. However, from the viewpoint of narcotics units, those locations may require difficult undercover operations or may only involve small amounts of drugs. Narcotics police tend to be more attentive to locations that yield large quantities of drugs and high arrest numbers—the traditional measures of success. They are sometimes accused of only fishing where the fish are big and hungry—or, in police parlance, "at the same old watering holes."

Divergent patrol and narcotics interests are more easily reconciled in SATCOM than in other boroughs. "Chief Dunne is a strong supporter of nuisance abatement," says David. "He is in a position to get patrol and narcotics to work together. He sets the tone." For Dunne, 100 Palmetto epitomized spiraling drug notoriety in search of a permanent solution. "We had to move on it; the precinct was more than receptive. They and Civil Enforcement did a yeoman job," recalled Dunne. David explains: "Our attorneys go to the field, meet with the precincts, and liaison with narcotics. Dunne's given us everything we need. It's made a big difference for us." The figures bear him out. In 1996, the CEU handled 709 nuisance abatement cases; of those, 217 were in SATCOM, which had the highest number of court-ordered closings among any of the boroughs.

Precinct Breakthroughs

SATCOM's precincts are the epicenters of operational intelligence. According to former SATCOM precinct commander Deputy Inspector Joseph Cuneen, "Under SATCOM, the narcotics supervisor reports directly to us about chronic drug locations, complaints, search warrants, and narcotics cases in our precinct. In the old days, the narcotics module [unit] would only send us a brief monthly report with some statistics on arrests." This observation touches upon an earlier era, when NYPD units would toil the same land but cling to their own harvests. Nowadays, detectives and narcotics units are more willing to work with patrol in developing strategies, debriefing prisoners, and developing search warrants. Cuneen recalled a recent incident: "We had shootings concentrated in one apartment building, and we knew they were drug related. Our precinct SNEU [Street Narcotics Enforcement Unit] secured warrants and made drug and other arrests along with narcotics [unit]. They worked with detectives in debriefing suspects and even secured three guns. Previously, narcotics would not know about shootings. Each unit would go their own way. You see detectives and police officers working on the same problem. It's great to see!"

Precinct commanders conduct their own crime strategy meetings to prepare for Dunnestat and Compstat meetings and implement new assignments. "I hold meetings with all my precinct supervisors to make sure that they're aware of everything going on and pass information on to the officers and the community," reports one experienced commanding officer. Inspector Judy McGinn, a SATCOM precinct commander, conducts meetings with "representatives of the various precinct investigative units to determine their progress and to offer strategies for emerging crime." Another SATCOM precinct commander holds pre- and post-Dunnestat meetings to focus on hot-spot locations. "I also question supervisors about recent crimes, specific shootings, and unusual robberies. They, in turn, tend to be more alert and aware of problem conditions," he says.

In addition, Dunnestat also circulates successful crime-fighting tips through the precinct circuit. When asked about the source of a new precinct anticrime tactic, COs rarely claim originality. Instead, they acknowledge Dunnestat and Compstat. "I brought home many ideas first learned at the borough," recounted a precinct commander. The ideas included "vehicle checkpoints with covered escape routes, fingerprinting recovered autos, use of cell phones to conduct warrant checks from the field, and immediate warrant and background checks of victims of shootings and other serious crimes." As an experienced precinct crime fighter, Inspector Joanne Jaffe pointed out: "The meetings have forced me to try to know everything that I can. If I have to know everything, I will make sure all my bosses and cops know everything, too."

Several precincts have adopted a strategy that originated in SATCOM's Crown Heights section. That community and its 77th Precinct were distressed by drug-dealing havens masquerading as legitimate storefront businesses. In September 1996 the precinct's Community Policing Unit (CPU) launched an approach to supplement nuisance abatement and other antidrug strategies. Sergeant Guy Bouillon and his CPU team researched city and state laws related to opening and operating a business. After collaborating with and obtaining approval from SATCOM, headquarters, and the Brooklyn district attorney's office, the team examined more than 100 business location kites (drug complaints), from which it selected 29 sites. Operation Close Out checked these businesses for observance of consumer, health, fire, and tax codes; certificates of occupancy and business; and beer licenses. Within four months, 117 locations were inspected for violations, and 90 were closed. Numerous summonses and several felony arrests accompanied the action. Between the program's launch in September 1996 and October 20, 1997, the precinct's major crimes declined 40 percent. The precinct commander, Captain Ronald Wasson, enlisted the community to try to ensure that landlords rented only to legitimate businesses. Community Board Chairman Robert Matthews reported: "They are doing an excellent job. They have taken the bad elements out of our neighborhood, and we applaud their work."[30] "Close Out" was such a success that Commander Wasson prepared a detailed program booklet that included illustrations of relevant codes, laws, and forms. This was distributed to all precinct commanders.

Conclusion: Sustaining SATCOM

SATCOM spawned new approaches. The infamous 100 Palmetto Street, for example, was one of the very few city residential (as opposed to commercial) drug addresses to be closed through the nuisance abatement law. SATCOM's Palmetto strike and Operation Close Out embody the intersection of problem solving and community policing, fueled by swiftly shared information, energetic leadership, streamlined operations, mobile cops, and additional resources. SATCOM bolsters Compstat's ability to monitor strategies and tactics; the devil is indeed in the details.

SATCOM dramatically showcased an "X factor": As narcotics arrests increased, crime dramatically decreased. Since SATCOM, the NYPD has launched major antidrug offensives in other boroughs. While the fanfare has resembled that for SATCOM, the command structures have not. Major Manhattan, Bronx, and Queens narcotics initiatives, for example, resemble SATCOM's antidrug campaign but not its geographically based organizational and managerial arrangements.

If SATCOM is so successful, why has it not been in the vanguard of subsequent NYPD reform? Has it failed to live up to its billing by the former police commissioner William Bratton as "the professional envy of the world"? Has it not fulfilled its designation by Chief Anemone as a "management laboratory, a smarter way of doing business . . . a signature piece . . . the NYPD's boldest attack on narcotics"? Without offspring, a program like SATCOM could ultimately fail to thrive.

Facile Answers.   Some explanations for the NYPD's failure to duplicate SATCOM are deceptively seductive. While SATCOM's 1996 record was extraordinary, the argument goes, its subsequent crime reduction was not. SATCOM slid in 1997. Its steep 1996 crime rate drop of almost 20 percent declined to less than half that figure, or 10 percent, barely exceeding the 1997 citywide drop of 9 percent. While in 1996 it held first place, in 1997 two other patrol boroughs outpaced SATCOM'S crime drop.[31] On the other hand, the city's 1997 crime rate declined less steeply in every borough. In addition, the two boroughs that slightly out-performed SATCOM received departmental priority and major infusions of narcotics cops in 1997. SATCOM, moreover, was a victim of its own success. Its impressive successes after April 1996 made it far more difficult to reduce crime further in 1997. The graph below displays SATCOM's diminishing post-April 1997 monthly crime drop compared to the other boroughs.

SATCOM's ability to preserve and extend its 1996 drop in crime into the following year appears quite remarkable. This was accomplished with diminished resources. NYPD press releases, speeches, and newspaper accounts heralded a total of 800 SAT-COM narcotics officers, but that total was never realized. According to NYPD records, SATCOM reached its peak in July 1997 with 722 narcotics officers before steadily declining and then leveling off throughout most of the rest of 1997 at around 475. But SATCOM missed more than mass; it also lost key people to other NYPD operations, most notably in Manhattan.

Before 1996 ended, the NYPD drug spotlight shifted to three upper-Manhattan precincts at the foot of the George Washing-

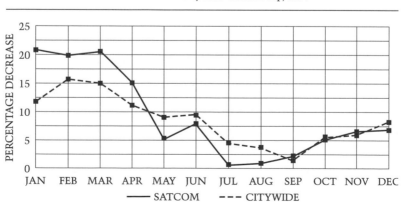

SATCOM vs. Citywide Crime Drop, 1997

ton Bridge, which links Manhattan to New Jersey and facilitates drive-by drug sales. Brazen New York and East Coast wholesale drug dealing had long ravaged the area's communities. The Manhattan NYPD narcotics war was headed mostly by newly appointed generals, many of whom were seasoned warriors from the SATCOM antidrug campaign. The Manhattan North Initiative (MNI) not only used some SATCOM narcotics officers but also borrowed some tactics. In many ways, subsequent campaigns have been bound to Brooklyn even if their "lineage" was hushed. The NYPD has improved in many ways, but developing a willingness to acknowledge previous contributions is not one of them.

A *Closer Look*. Dwindling SATCOM resources and changing NYPD targets provide a window on NYPD politics and reforms. In addition, personnel transfers in the byzantine NYPD are a constant. For all its presumed autonomy, SATCOM is part of a larger bureaucratic labyrinth laid out not merely for crime reduction but also for career advancement. The lines between the two are often fuzzy. Thus, the durability of the SATCOM Brooklyn North design as a geographically based operation with sufficient resources is not assured. But should it be? Or are other strategies and managerial modes preferable in similar or different neighborhoods? Unfortunately, NYPD scorekeeping changes frequently. Inadequate measures of success and shifting criteria not only reduce clarity, they blur one's ability to steer change. Innocent people are not the only victims of crime stories; truth also suffers. Inspecting the blend of bureaucratic sparring, managerial vision, changeable values, and shifting standards provides the best "handle" on reform's chances. This analysis follows.

8   NEW SKYLINE

First Rule of Holes: When you are in one, you should stop digging.
—Molly Ivins [1]

The reduction of crime in New York City continues to get good reviews. As important as New York's crime abatement is, it is not the main focus of this book. Rather, I have sought to answer the following question: If pre-1994 NYPD reform movements were short-lived and cyclical, what is it about today's NYPD that may keep it vibrant and one step ahead of crime? Decentralization, greater accountability, and a flattened hierarchy—issues that typically dominate the current bureaucratic reform agenda—are not new. What is new since 1994 is the setting in place of unusual engines of organizational change within the NYPD. This change has been sustained not just by strong leadership but through the dynamics of intelligence-led policing. And it is this informed decision making that is the focus of this book.

The NYPD currently is breaking out of its old bunker mentality, which has been "when in doubt, dig deeper." Police departments have traditionally been shackled by outdated ideas, such as the belief that a rapid, beefed-up response to crime incidents reduces crime. When more cops and radio car runs did nothing to stop rising crime rates, the police sought refuge in social and economic explanations. The former high-ranking chief James Hannon noted, "There were blocks in the city so bad—where rocks were thrown off roofs at the cops—that the department simply did not send anyone into them; they stationed patrol cars at either end instead."[2] Such sections of the city with impoverished conditions, entrenched unemployment, and long-standing animosity toward the police were written off.

Since 1994, however, the NYPD has made structural changes in the ways it looks at and deals with crime. The current NYPD mind-set contrasts starkly with that of previous eras. One police analyst remembered, "The department of 1982, despite its changes at the top, seemed to be working very much like the police department of 1976. . . . [I]t was a well-oiled machine and the chiefs were all more or less interchangeable . . . as long as they stayed honest and were committed to a clean and nonviolent department."[3]

"Well-oiled" and innovative can represent opposite ends of a spectrum. Today's young cast of precinct commanders and higher-echelon officers sharply differs from previous decades when "it was only after reaching retirement status, after putting in your twenty years, that you began climbing the appointive ranks. That was why the police department's 'young tigers' were well into middle age."[4] Risk takers in the old days received less organizational encouragement than they do today. To make matters worse, the crime workload far exceeded the current number of cases. Manhattan alone had 661 homicides in 1972, more than all of New York City in 1998. As recently as 1993, there were more than 600,000 felonies committed in the city; 1998 will see under 300,000 felonies—a very significant drop.

Yet, as this book has shown, it was the police administrations of those high-crime years that prepared the ground for today's new structure. Increased decentralization, enhanced supervision, and greater command accountability and authority have been NYPD reform themes for more than a century. And although these ambitious aims have proven elusive or transitory, they have had a residual, if not a cumulative, effect.

Robert McGuire, commissioner for almost six years (1978–1983) and one of the longest-serving modern-day commissioners, could still observe five years after Commissioner Patrick Murphy departed, "We are trying to reverse a trend. We want the area commanders and the precinct captains to take more responsibility. We have to let them see they're not going to get hurt if they make their own decisions."[5]

In the 1990s, Commissioner Lee Brown's community policing program advocated mini–police chiefs within the department responsible for their particular communities. One observer heralded Brown's arrival with an optimistic forecast: He "has creative ideas about policing . . . [d]ecentralizing the police bureaucracy, reemphasizing the importance of the cop on the beat (as opposed to those in patrol cars and special units), reestablishing a sense of law and order in neighborhoods that have teetered on the brink of anarchy for decades."[6]

If many post-1993 reform impulses differ little from previous attempts, what accounts for their greater success? The answer is twofold. The first reason is firm external backing. The strong political support from Mayor Giuliani was a *sine qua non*. The mayor propelled many of the forces for change, and he stood by them. There were occasions when commanders complained to their community political leaders that they felt mistreated at Compstat meetings. When the politicos in turn complained to the mayor, he did not back off. Giuliani's close relationship with Commissioner Howard Safir has also been critical to NYPD success. The second essential factor is the successful convergence of information and decisions in Compstat meetings.

Intelligence-Led Policing

I have become an addict of sorts—a Compstat junkie, having attended well over 100 headquarters and borough Compstat meetings, as well as miniprecinct meetings and numerous precinct-related activities. And it seems the more you look, the more you find, the more you learn, the more you want to see, and the more there is to learn.

The lessons of Compstat are there for practitioners and researchers alike, as the old divisions between them erode and common areas of interest come together. The NYPD, assisted by the National Institute of Justice (NIJ) and others, has fostered an unprecedented sharing of information—both internally and among law enforcement organizations and students of policing.

Quickly bringing the right information to bear on police decisions, or on any decisions, for that matter, is not a novel notion. Over fifty years ago, a young social scientist and future Nobel Prize winner diagnosed the malfunctioning of large organizations. Long before Tom Peters, James Champy, and other modern-day management gurus unleashed the curative powers of downsizing, flattening, empowerment, and reengineering, Herbert Simon examined the managerial elixirs of the 1940s.[7] The management approaches of that period were based on certain principles of administration that were considered universally applicable. Simon demonstrated how some of these principles—unity of command, task specialization, hierarchical arrangements, and increased numbers of people reporting to a supervisor—clash operationally and work at cross-purposes. He posited that all decisions are composite decisions, arising from "informational premises" and can be traced through formal and informal channels of communication.[8]

Particular administrative and managerial arrangements make sense only when they provide key decision makers with the appropriate and timely "premises" necessary for decisions. Therefore, every supervisory and managerial arrangement in the organization must be customized to support the decision makers' informational needs.

The NYPD has made enormous strides in feeding information to appropriate decision-making levels. Traditionally, NYPD headquarters was perceived as the nerve center of the department's decision-making apparatus. Changes in operational police tactics were conceived, formulated, and issued from headquarters, primarily on a citywide basis, and often with very little input from field commands. The post-1993 restructuring and crime-control strategies provided field commanders with far more leverage over their own troops. The changes also required the formation of teams designed to break down the informational barriers separating the generalists assigned to the patrol divisions from specialized units such as the Detective Bureau and Organized Crime Control Bureau. Citywide specialty units such as the Street Crime Unit and the School Program to Educate and Control Drug Abuse (SPECDA) were subdivided, and their personnel reassigned to boroughs.

The post-1993 NYPD leadership also realized that uniform, citywide crime-fighting decisions were not as effective as individualized strategies designed for particular communities. One precinct anticrime supervisor explained that a plainclothes unit in midtown Manhattan could easily follow a suspect on foot or by car without being detected, whereas the police unit would immediately be identified on the far less populated streets of Brooklyn.

By increasing the authority and responsibility of precinct commanders, the NYPD freed them from having to forward information along the chain of command simply to receive high-level confirmation or reassurance.

Information from headquarters is no longer released to units only on a "need-to-know" basis, or maintained solely by specialized units. Precincts have become not only sources of information but also centers for rapid decision making based on first-hand analyses of crime data.

Strategic Information

Post-1993 strategy documents publicly acknowledge the failure of previous crime-fighting initiatives that were introduced on an incremental basis in isolated units or geographic areas. New administrative positions have been created to facilitate the flow of information within the NYPD. For example, Strategy Number Four, "Breaking the Cycle of Domestic Violence," directed precincts to designate a "Domestic Violence Prevention Officer," charged with gathering and maintaining precinct domestic violence information. This officer was responsible for monitoring the status of cases through a review of departmental records and personal contacts (such as home visits, correspondence, phone calls, and station house interviews). One of the officer's major functions was to identify any locations requiring special attention. Domestic violence investigators were also named in each precinct detective squad to investigate open complaints and identify patterns of abuse.

In addition to creating entirely new information sources, the strategies transferred some units and positions, again for the purpose of coordination of information. One Narcotics Division unit, for example, was assigned to work with homicide detectives to make connections between murders and illegal drug activity. For the connections to be of help, information had to be accurate and timely. Strategy Number Four, for example, introduced the "Domestic Violence Incident Report," so that alerted patrol officers would record their responses to domestic incidents. Such data are fed into a "Domestic Incident Database" to supply critical information regarding past violent episodes, existing orders of protection, and outstanding warrants for household members. A new police database of "Chronic Emotionally Disturbed Persons" was put together to aid responders, the courts, and medical practitioners in identifying individuals with a history of violent encounters.

At the end of 1996, Commissioner Safir unveiled a detailed strategy to reduce the numbers of persons who avoid prosecution by failing to appear before the courts. The strategy, "Bringing Fugitives to Justice,"[9] creates and utilizes more systematic informational databases to apprehend those who jump bail, disobey the terms of their parole or probation, or ignore appearance tickets or summonses. The strategy calls for compiling and prioritizing lists of fugitives wanted for serious crimes or narcotics offenses and coordinates efforts to apprehend them.

The vital link between information and crime fighting as demonstrated by the NYPD is receiving worldwide attention. The University of Maryland criminologist Charles F. Wellford found that the most important factor leading to the solution of a murder case is the swift notification of a homicide detective by the officer at the crime scene. Other critical information comes from running checks on guns, interviewing witnesses, and performing computer checks on witnesses and suspects. Taken together, these factors accurately predict the disposition of 99 percent of homicide cases.[10]

A movement in the United Kingdom called "intelligence-led policing" recognizes information's key role. This approach involves more refined police tactics, deployments, and strategies geared toward ensuring that all members of the force are in the right place with the right information. One strategy encourages the lowest level, British street bobbies (constables), to become more involved in solving major crimes because they are often in possession of vital community information.[11] While teaching at the Police Staff College in Bramshill, Hampshire, England, I learned of a constable who, as part of this new emphasis on total involvement and the sharing of information, was able (through his intimate knowledge of local conditions) to provide the key to locating a missing child who had diabetes.

Compstat Intelligence

The NYPD and organizations emulating its successes are undergoing a revolutionary change—a new way of relating to their environment. As NIJ Director Jeremy Travis writes:

> The new forms of policing that have emerged in recent years view crime as problems to be solved, not simply as an event to which the police react. The community is viewed as a partner in this effort, not merely as a collection of witnesses to be canvassed after the event and a public to be informed about police issues.[12]

The ability of police to function in this new way depends on their having access to accurate information and a mechanism for the coordinated use of that information.

Compstat has been the informational cement of reform, the central mechanism that provides communication links to traditionally isolated specialized units. Fragmentation is not unique to the NYPD. It plagues all large police departments and most large organizations. The Harvard management expert Rosabeth Kanter calls it "segmentalism" and notes, "The failure of many organization-change efforts has more to do with the lack . . . of an integrating, institutionalizing mechanism than with inherent problems in an innovation itself."[13] Without Compstat, fragmentation would continue to rule supreme. Compstat's confrontation of informational splintering is indispensable to the NYPD's organizational well-being.

Sorting Out Compstat

Compstat's multidimensional qualities have positioned it as the catalyst of change within the NYPD. Compstat's beauty lies in its diversity. Informational, "need-to-know" crime stats have expanded into a multifunctional vessel for management planning and coordination.

As a management tool, Compstat has extended beyond crime fighting. Commissioner Safir uses it to monitor and address civilian complaints of misconduct against members of the police department. Compstat now includes citywide, borough, and precinct data by hour and time of day for FADO (force, abuse, discourtesy, and obscene language) citizen complaints.

It is no secret that questions have been raised about whether the new policing, with its assertive pursuit of low-level crime, actually encourages incidents of FADO—most dramatically illustrated by the terrible incident involving a Haitian immigrant, Abner Louima. On August 9, 1997, Louima was allegedly tortured, sodomized, and brutalized by four NYPD officers inside a police precinct when a wooden stick was shoved in his rectum and then his mouth. Louima had to wait an hour before he was taken to a hospital, where physician records document severe internal damage to his intestines and bladder. Fortunately, the incident triggered the arrest of four officers, the suspension of several others, and the transfer of still more officers, including the commanding officer of the precinct, who was on vacation at the time. The incident also led to the creation of a special mayoral task force, an inquiry into the effectiveness of the existing civilian complaint review board, the involvement of federal prosecutors, and an examination of the extent to which this incident was indicative of a pattern of police brutality. Commissioner Safir's FADO mechanism, along with the other measures just described, strongly suggests that the new policing is a force against, not in favor of, police brutality.

Nevertheless, safeguarding the rights of all citizens requires constant vigilance and scrutiny. Controversy erupted after the February 1999 killing of an unarmed West African street peddler in the foyer of his Bronx apartment building. Four white members of the NYPD's elite Street Crime Unit (SCU) fired forty-one times. Amadou Diallo, who had arrived from Guinea almost three years earlier and had no criminal record, was struck by nineteen bullets. The critics have every right to complain, but they have it wrong. It is not racism; it is not insensitive white cops systematically singling out minorities because of their ethnicity and color. What the police are doing is more of what they've been doing, and that is the real problem.

The NYPD's dramatic and highly successful onslaught on crime is rooted in the department's eagerness to examine crime critically and mount innovative, targeted crime-fighting approaches. If citizen trust and intelligence are critical to crime fighting, then the department is in danger of losing vital sources of information if it increases enforcement activities without regard to the community. For example, the strong nexus that the department uncovered between drugs and crime in Brooklyn North (see Chapter 7) is now being targeted in other boroughs, requiring a substantial increase in narcotics officers throughout the city. Even though the force has grown, it is not yet large enough to support the rising number of undercover narcotics officers, many of whom are being drawn from street patrol and other units. Although crime has gone down throughout the city, the decreasing uniformed presence intensifies public anxiety.

Policing involves both negative and positive citizen contact. When the negative far outweighs the positive, public confidence declines. The SCU, involved in the tragic Diallo shooting, has been highly successful in harvesting guns from the street, no doubt thereby decreasing violent crime. But more intensified police action is necessary to recover the dwindling number of street guns. Ratcheting up the pressure leads to more searches at the margins and possible mistakes, which rob the public of its sense of security and trust. In addition, the recent rapid expansion of the undercover SCU inevitably affects quality control and further drains the visible police force. Similarly, many community police officers—key citizen connectors—are being shifted to narcotics and other specialized units, further diminishing police visibility and public confidence.

We expect a lot from our police: enforce the law, reduce crime, and honor the rights of all citizens. In the last several years, the NYPD has been quite innovative in navigating these often conflicting currents. New times require a new commitment to innovative policing. Fear of police should not replace fear of crime.

Compstat Myths.   Exploring some Compstat myths and misleading assumptions helps to spotlight its multidimensional qualities.

MYTH NUMBER ONE: Compstat is nothing more than up-to-date information—knowing what the level of crime is and when and where it is happening.

Response: Yes, Compstat is up-to-date crime information, which for many years was absent in the department. But it took vision to see the value and potential in these crime statistics, and confidence and a "can-do" mentality to believe that the police could do something about crime. The need and ability to know about the extent of crime and the events related to it had to precede the ability to manage crime. And it took creativity and diligence to establish a system to capture crime complaints and arrest activities. Primitive by today's standards, the first Compstat book later evolved into more refined and sophisticated versions. Compstat insiders refer to their first year as "spring training," a period of "tryouts and team building before the season began in earnest." [14]

MYTH NUMBER TWO: The only major difference between Compstat and approaches taken by other police departments is the use of sophisticated computer technologies and software mapping capabilities that complement statistical analyses and deployment data.

Response: The transformation of pin-mapping to computer mapping and other technological advances were unquestionably important. However, their value would not have been so pervasive without the injection of Compstat into the department's bloodstream.

Compstat coordinates operations through the consistent review of various strategies. In the past, for example, a drug operation such as Operation Pressure Point would not be systematically and simultaneously observed for its impact on adjoining precincts. The examination of maps by all relevant participants is extremely important in addressing the complexity of the city and its neighborhoods. Compstat facilitates both uniform crime strategies applicable to all areas and special approaches.

A good case in point was a creative approach to bicycles, which, beginning about 1996, were used in robberies, shootings, and drug transactions. A commanding officer identified laws regulating the operation of bicycles. Through lawful bicycle inspections, enforcement swept up nineteen guns within that one precinct by the end of the summer. This success was heralded at a Compstat meeting and resulted in a citywide adoption of this strategy. The approach has subsequently resulted in the confiscation of hundreds of guns and large quantities of narcotics from this previously "invisible" criminal element.

MYTH NUMBER THREE: Compstat is just a crime strategy meeting. What is so innovative about having police officials focus on reducing crime?

Response: Compstat meetings represent a pioneering assemblage of multiple sources of information before all key NYPD and criminal justice agencies. Compstat coordinates the activities of parole and probation officials, district attorneys, corrections personnel, and other law enforcement groups. In years past, other concerns were considered more pressing—minimizing scandals, maintaining community well-being, and preserving a low police profile.

MYTH NUMBER FOUR: There are some who argue that Compstat is irrelevant to the way the police reduce crime. "It's a matter of priorities," reported one columnist.[15] They argue that the attacks on quality-of-life crimes and the department's "zero tolerance" policy have had the greatest impact on crime.

Response: Of course, police priorities and practices count. But through Compstat they are continually reviewed so that they can be revised as needed. Compstat helps the department assess the rigor and effectiveness of its crime strategies regarding quality of life, reclaiming public spaces, the Civil Enforcement Initiative, the nature of detective debriefings of arrestees, and the search for accomplices involved in particular crime incidents.

MYTH NUMBER FIVE: Compstat, after all, is only the application of modern management approaches and techniques, which ensure that precinct commanders are held accountable for results and are given the tools and authority to achieve these results. What is new about this? We have been hearing about these concepts since the turn of the century.

Response: Compstat is certainly a modern management tool to ensure commander accountability. And it is true that since the early 1900s, public officials and academics have been stressing the need to give executives authority commensurate with responsibility.

What the naysayers of Compstat fail to take into account is that change is not on autopilot, especially in a large, hierarchically structured organization. As practitioners and students of complex organizations know, change requires constant application through systematic reinforcing mechanisms.

MYTH NUMBER SIX: Compstat generates disagreement and conflict among different units of the department. This effect is detrimental, since stories (some accurate, some not) of conflict spread quickly and can demoralize participants.

Response: Compstat does not generate disagreement and conflict within the police department as much as it *reveals* them. This is a functional, not dysfunctional, aspect of the organization. Conflict and disagreement within various units are inevitable and can provide the grist for change. The Compstat quest for integration never ends; it is constantly pursued. Change is not painless, however. Organizations need to be committed to and open to learning.

Compstat: Double-Loop Learning

As police scholar Herman Goldstein observed, organizational change is multidimensional.[16] As an agent of change, Compstat has generated key NYPD reform processes such as new strategies, reengineering, and reorganization. Compstat has also been, to a large extent, the organizational glue that has bonded many of the changes together. Compstat operates on three major levels. Like the tip of an iceberg, the top level—informational sources and analyses—is most visible to the observer. One must be fairly close to the policing process to view the second layer, management and planning. And the bottom layer, organizational learning, which constitutes the structural base for the other two layers, is the least visible. Yet this layer tends to generate the most change. As often is the case, the hidden may be the most profound.

Constant Experimentation.   A great deal of Compstat's activity falls under the heading of what organizational theorists call "double-loop learning."[17] This contrasts with single-loop learning (the predominant mode in most organizations), which involves the detection and correction of error, enabling an organization to continue with or achieve its policies and objectives. Double-loop learning, on the other hand, is more rare and involves questioning basic operating assumptions, entertaining disparate approaches, and experimenting with different arrangements. This experimental approach is reflected in many Compstat efforts, such as SATCOM–Brooklyn North and the Manhattan North Initiative (MNI), which are competing organizational and managerial arrangements devoted to different major antidrug efforts.

Critical Thinking. Compstat meetings discover difficulties and obstacles, defend positions, debunk the past and discard existing practices, demand ownership or responsibility, diagnose problems, design alternative strategies, deploy resources, delegate and coordinate responsibilities, devolve authority, disseminate information, and, finally, define and deliver solutions.

Coterie of Dedicated Staff. The Compstat process includes an extremely committed and imaginative staff. The Compstat office not only prepares for and analyzes meetings and data but also develops new Compstat informational components and issues. Remove the Compstat office from the chief of department's office, and you remove a substantial portion of its influence on reform.

Creative Problem Solving. Compstat is the forum where new problem-solving approaches are often presented, reviewed, analyzed, reexamined, and circulated. Many of these solutions are first developed at the precinct level. Operation Close Out, which was first tested in the 77th Precinct, provides a classic example of Compstat's problem-solving approach in terms of origination, diagnosis, classification, and the presentation of alternative solutions (see Chapter 7).

Continuity and Consistency. On a number of levels, Compstat is the central mechanism for the articulation of its own four-part mantra—accurate and timely intelligence, effective tactics, rapid deployment, and relentless and consistent follow-up, with particular emphasis on follow-up and constant monitoring.

Rarely noted aspects of Compstat's continuity and consistency are the regularity of its meetings and the commitment of attendees. The adoption of a regular schedule was a conscious decision made at the outset. It was based on the belief that Compstat would not be taken seriously by the troops if it met only occasionally. When a police officer was shot the night before a meeting in 1995, the 7:00 A.M. meeting still took place the next day. Headquarters and top-level borough participants rarely miss meetings, sustaining Compstat's continuity and consistency. Events, incidents, and discussions raised at one Compstat meeting are recorded, remembered, and revisited by these participants at subsequent meetings.

Control.   While Compstat and other departmental innovations have placed some responsibility, accountability, and decision making at the borough and precinct levels, where they are most appropriate, the top-level officers have not lost control. Authority is still exercised at the top, but it is now a more informed version of control based on results, not just activities. When subordinates are evaluated, more emphasis is placed on crime rate declines than on such activities as arrests and radio car responses. These statistics still count, but they count in terms of their relationship to results, a reversal of previous policies.

Central Nervous System.   Compstat serves as a thermometer of organizational well-being. If things go wrong or information is not being shared, the problem probably will emerge at some point at a Compstat meeting. The flow of a meeting can be interrupted when it becomes apparent that previous department directives (for example, distributing equipment from headquarters units to the field) have not been carried out.

Center Stage.   Whether or not a patrol officer has ever attended a Compstat meeting, he or she is likely to have an opinion about Compstat. At the precinct level, Compstat meetings are known as the place where precinct commanders are grilled on crime-reduction efforts. This impression reinforces the patrol officer's desire to combat crime. Precinct commanders occasionally bring precinct officers who have performed a heroic feat to a Compstat meeting, where they are applauded for their accomplishment. The fact that Compstat has been noted at least twice on the television show *NYPD Blue* illustrates how its reputation has reached into popular culture.

Reframing Reform

The future course of reform hinges on several factors. The first is the need for reform champions—strong and energetic advocates who control resources. Although reform has been substantially advanced, it is never securely anchored. The former commissioner William Bratton's claim of *turnaround*[18] in the NYPD is not the same as "stay around." Bratton's recent observation that the department is on some sort of autopilot for further crime reduction "as a direct result of the systems we put in place"[19] understates the dynamics of reform. Systems do not operate independently of people taking action; they must be periodically changed and upgraded.

Previous reform efforts disintegrated once their vigilant champions left the scene. There is no reason to believe that the present is any different. Regardless of the nature of structural reform, there is also a visceral quality to police leadership. Cops need leaders who connect with the job, who are really there. Commissioner Safir's advancement in rank of vigorous reform advocates shows an understanding of this principle—that to be a leader is to be a connector, an energizer.

Reform will also depend on continued Compstat creativity. Despite denials, serious consideration at the top echelons was given to decentralizing Compstat and replacing most headquarters meetings with borough Compstat meetings. In 1998, there was a seven-week headquarters Compstat experiment in which the borough leaders were substituted for the top brass as the lead questioners. The quality of questioning varied, depending on the borough leadership.

In addition to continuing to shift operational responsibility to lower levels, effective borough Compstats could help deal with a long-standing NYPD problem: inadequate middle-level supervision. Repeated corruption and other scandals have revealed middle-level supervision as the fragile link in the chain of command. Despite the flattening of its hierarchical pyramid, the NYPD is still a large, thick bureaucracy. Addressing supervisory issues at the borough level makes sense.

Compstat and Communities

Long-lasting reform requires reaching out. The NYPD is learning that police action taken to reduce crime means little without constructive citizen contact and cooperation. Commissioner Safir has made encouraging moves in this direction. If precincts have an excessive number of complaints about abuse or discourtesy, commanders are queried at Compstat about how they are handling problem officers. The more this practice is developed and made known to the community, the stronger community ties will become.

An NYPD strategy issued in August 1997 forthrightly acknowledges that "whatever gains we have achieved in fighting crime are minimized if the price is the trust and respect of the community we serve."[20] This strategy seeks to incorporate courtesy, professionalism, and respect (CPR) through updated recruitment processes, executive development, officer training, monitoring of street behavior, Compstat review, and strengthened citizen involvement.

Community outreach, however, means far more. Public alliances, as George Kelling and Catherine Coles persuasively demonstrate, can pay huge dividends.[21] Harvard Public Health Professor Felton Earls noted, "Police work may help troubled neighborhoods. This could be the leading edge of greater change because reduced crime brings neighborhood life under better control."[22] The department has been working more closely with communities, and there are several encouraging signs.

For years the Washington Heights section of Manhattan served as the center of wholesale drug traffic for New York and the entire East Coast. Lying at the foot of the George Washington Bridge, the area was easily accessed from Upper Manhattan and New Jersey. West 163rd Street, between Broadway and Saint Nicholas Avenue, was the hub of this drug distribution. Gang leaders presided over an apartment building on the block by terrorizing legitimate tenants, "sometimes firing weapons indiscriminately and sometimes earning $70,000 a week in high-volume sales of small packages of cocaine and marijuana."[23] They also controlled two storefronts in a building on 163rd Street. The dealers spray-painted hallways to mark where drugs could be purchased and left threatening messages. The vacant apartments in the tenement building had become "a maze of traps, meant to block out . . . rivals and the police. Electrified wires had been stretched across window frames and holes had been smashed in walls and floors to provide easy escape routes. Hallway floors had been smeared with Vaseline to trip up unwary intruders."[24] Drivers and pedestrians were solicited and harassed on the street.

The NYPD launched a major antinarcotics project, the Northern Manhattan Initiative (NMI), in the fall of 1996 to shut down this criminal activity and help residents take back their neighborhood—if necessary, piece-by-piece, a block at a time. Eleven months later, intelligence gathering and law enforcement on 163rd Street resulted in what the *Boston Globe* characterized as a "virtual invasion" by the police.[25] By arresting and removing gang members, padlocking two gang-affiliated storefronts (through a nuisance abatement procedure), sealing off vacant apartments, and securing the targeted block, the police effectively shut down drug dealing, though some civil-liberties advocates voiced their outrage.[26] One officer, remembering the intensity of the situation, said, "We had lists of suspected drug locations on the block, and every building on that list you went into, you were going to come out with somebody who was either buying or dealing drugs."[27]

What followed was a textbook case of community policing. The department realized that dismantling one major drug organization does not prevent its replacement by another, especially when there are affluent customer bases in adjoining suburban Westchester County and New Jersey. "We're not going to put a Band-Aid on the problem," said precinct commander Garry McCarthy.[28] For the next three months, the department maintained a twenty-four-hours-a-day, seven-days-a-week presence, with uniformed police and established checkpoints on both ends of the block. Motorists attempting to enter the area were questioned by officers who had been designated as "point men" to choke off drive-by drug purchases. Deputy Commissioner George Grasso, who is in charge of NYPD legal matters, said, "We have designed this in a way where everyone's rights are protected. Residents have a right to live in a safe environment."[29]

People living in the neighborhood enrolled in the Trespass Affidavit Program: Residents signed a document giving the police permission to question and search anyone who entered their premises. The NYPD enlisted the help of numerous city agencies, including Sanitation, Parks, Transportation, Fire, Public Health, and Consumer Affairs, plus the New York City Chapter of the American Society for the Prevention of Cruelty to Animals. Streets were cleaned, abandoned cars were towed, potholes were filled, graffiti on walls and street lamps was painted over, and trees were planted.

Community mobilization followed. A community meeting attracted a record 300 attendees. Residents expressed increased confidence in the area's safety and in the police. The police formed a block association, a tenant association in each building, and a youth council. Tenant groups began patrolling each building, and citizens volunteered as block watchers. Landlords granted the newly formed tenant associations first right of refusal to new renters who they believed might be involved in the drug trade. The community vigorously responded to the NYPD's invitation to participate actively.

Crime has plunged dramatically. Before the gang was removed, there were twenty-seven major crimes on the block in nine months. In the next nine months, only four crimes occurred there. As McCarthy described police strategy, "We're trying to effect a long-term solution to something that has plagued this neighborhood, and still does. If we have to do it block-by-block, so be it."[30] Perhaps even more telling is a comment by eighty-eight-year-old community activist John Matthews, Sr., regarding a Christmas tree that stood outside in the neighborhood, untouched for five weeks: "Nobody took a light or a bulb or anything."[31]

New York City's community policing, in the words of criminal-justice expert Jerome McElroy, "has apparently served enough time in purgatory" and is reemerging. The NYPD highlighted the "Model Block Program," as it came to be known and replicated elsewhere in the city, in its second annual Compstat conference, which drew hundreds of people from around the world. It is instructive that this 1998 conference was called "Compstat and Community Policing." In addition to McCarthy, seven other commanding officers recounted their activities in a session called "Problem Solving and Community Oriented Policing in the NYPD."

Inspector Edward Cannon, for example, the 75th Precinct's respected, crime-fighting commanding officer, presides over one of the city's most populous and busiest precincts. With a population of more than 161,000 people in 5.5 square miles, police dispatchers at this East New York section of Brooklyn receive between 95,000 and 100,000 radio calls annually. For years, Cannon has worked closely with the community. "Prevention and deterrence of crime is the goal," said Cannon. "The premise is simple—a very small number of criminals are doing a very large number of crimes." Cannon's multipronged strategies, which involves constantly mobilizing community groups, paid off with a 43 percent reduction in robberies in 1997 compared to 1993; 175 fewer persons were shot, and 91 fewer people were murdered.

Missing Intelligence

Since 1993, old and new NYPD strategies have swiftly combined to produce an avalanche of change. The department, however, is not positioned to objectively determine the factors most critical to its successes. Using SATCOM Brooklyn North as an example, the following criteria could be factored into that command's success: effective leadership, additional resources, innovative organization and management groupings, and high-intensity tactics. Brooklyn North advocates assert that its unique geo-based organization and managerial arrangements are the main reasons for its exemplary record. Headquarters, patrol, narcotics, and detective leaders, on the other hand, assert that the infusion of additional narcotics and other officers is what fueled SATCOM's accomplishments.

The NYPD's systematic attempts to assess its own accomplishments have traditionally been scanty. In recent years, senior-level officials who, as mentioned in Chapter 3, attend the Columbia University Police Management Institute (PMI), are required to evaluate specialized projects and then to report to the commissioner and his senior executive staff. One PMI group analyzed SATCOM. The report cogently summarized and lauded the strengths of SATCOM and other major antidrug efforts, such as the Manhattan North Initiative, and also offered suggestions. But true to form, there were no objective comparative assessments.

Such sparse evaluation efforts should be no surprise. As social scientist James Q. Wilson has observed:

> No good idea will be seriously evaluated by anyone who has
> a patent on it. A test requires objectivity, technical skills, and
> a long time horizon. A practitioner is subjective (he or she must
> struggle to get the idea launched in an often hostile environ-

ment), is skilled at creating ideas but not necessarily at testing them, and has a time horizon shaped by tomorrow's newspaper story or next month's budget hearing, not by the two or three years that an adequate testing in the field involves.[32]

Headquarters' data monitoring scarcely makes its way into the department's operational mainstream. For several years, the Office of Management Analysis and Planning, under the enlightened leadership of Deputy Commissioner for Policy and Planning Michael J. Farrell, has tracked "certain key indicators of performance that reflect Department activity within the crime strategies." The report, *Action Indicators for Police Strategies*, for example, assesses the antigun strategy and provides comparative borough numbers on reports of shooting victims, shooting incidents, firearms search warrants, arrests for possession, and guns received. These figures compare current figures with last year's numbers and are distributed to all department chiefs. But many of the units are not acquainted with the report and its information.

Final Assessment

It has been said that criminologists aren't much better predictors than meteorologists.[33] That's a pity, because prediction is crucial. The NYPD asserts, "If you can predict it, you can prevent it."[34] This message reflects the department's post-1993 response to reducing crime. Following the department's lead, an assessment and a recommendation regarding the NYPD are in order.

Compstat reform has had a successful run. But no show runs forever. To forestall closing, Compstat requires constant rejuvenation. There are many possibilities: treating Compstat as a supervisory training mechanism; sending staff to Compstat college (described below); and using Compstat to improve CPR (courtesy, professionalism, and respect), citizen satisfaction, and community outreach. Without an aggressive drive to find new solutions and innovations to old problems, Compstat will become static, and reform will dwindle.

The NYPD can stay fresh and proactive through independent, objective analyses of its operation at different stages. If the NYPD sees itself as more than just a large police department, but instead as a laboratory for the benefit of police organizations everywhere—a testing ground in which innovations are successfully applied—it will help ensure Compstat's flourishing run.

This approach closely resembles what University of Maryland criminologist Lawrence Sherman labels "evidence-based policing." He proposes more "basic research on what works best when implemented properly under controlled conditions and ongoing outcomes research about the results each unit is actually achieving by applying or ignoring basic research in practice."[35] Sherman forcefully argues that closer linkages between research and practice will aid police strategies and problem solving.

Sherman praises Compstat for advancing "the results accountability principle farther than ever before," but he contends that Compstat "has not used the scientific method to assess cause and effect. Successful managers are rewarded, but successful methods are not pinpointed and codified."[36] Although, as this book has demonstrated, Compstat does pinpoint and codify successful methods quite well, it is true that assessments have not been done scientifically.

Of course, police departments do not exist in order to provide laboratories for social science research, but they can provide data for the benefit of both scholarship and practice. Missed evaluations are missed opportunities, especially when there are so many new initiatives.

A practical benefit of objective evaluations of the NYPD would be sharpened resource allocation. There are numerous models of optimum manpower distribution. Usually, however, the department bestows additional personnel to precinct, subway, or public housing areas where crime is rising or where influential constituents live. To its credit, Compstat is not tolerant when precinct commanders automatically respond "we need more people" to questions about below-par crime fighting. Yet, in some cases, insufficient or poorly used personnel may be the true explanations for crime spikes.

Compstat is good at examining police deployment but rarely reviews staffing levels of comparable precincts. Consider the scenario where Precinct A is more productive than comparable precincts with similar staffing levels. Perhaps Precinct A deserves even more resources to multiply its effectiveness. These types of analyses rarely enter the resource-allocation process. They would enhance the impact of hard information and possibly decrease bureaucratic infighting.

Today's police departments share knowledge and information on a scale far broader than ever before; the NYPD has been the source of much of this organizational restructuring. Compstat embodies the spirit and actions of many reformers seeking to make their groups more manageable and accountable—to deliver what is promised. It is not surprising that correctional, educational, and other institutions have also explored Compstat.

Within the NYPD itself, there is a great deal of sharing. In spring 1998, the Police Academy launched a curriculum consisting of fifteen-week sessions of three hours a week in which savvy commanding officers (COs) share their crime-strategy experiences with new and soon-to-be COs. Compstat College, according to Dr. James O'Keefe, NYPD's director of training, is a way of "perpetuating the corporate culture" by featuring a specific crime strategy approach during each session. Instead of having new COs get "beat up" at Compstat meetings, observes O'Keefe, "we try to shorten their learning curve." Compstat College sessions are videotaped, and a *Crime Control Strategies Reference Guide* is provided to participants. The guide and seminar discussions also explore effective ways to organize, display, and present information at Compstat meetings. The goal is for the participants to arrive together at innovative crime strategies. Compstat is growing institutional offshoots.

In an age when societal forces seem inexorable and overwhelming and the collective action of professionals often seems inconsequential, the NYPD has by most accounts made an enormous contribution to the city's well-being. Reflected in the city's polished image is its newest commodity, policing strategies that transform the way organizations gather and use information. This revolution in "blue" may resonate for decades as a profound contribution from the city that has no bounds. Today, the sun rising above the World Trade Center could well be emblematic of a city experiencing a renaissance, the New York of the twenty-first century.

APPENDIX A
NYPD Strategy Documents

Strategy Number One, "Getting Guns off the Streets of New York" (March 7, 1994).

Strategy Number Two, "Curbing Youth Violence in the Schools and on the Street" (April 6, 1994).

Strategy Number Three, "Driving Drug Dealers Out of New York" (April 6, 1994).

Strategy Number Four, "Breaking the Cycle of Domestic Violence" (April 26, 1994).

Strategy Number Five, "Reclaiming the Public Spaces of New York" (July 18, 1994).

Strategy Number Six, "Reducing Auto Related Crime in New York" (February 19, 1995).

Strategy Number Seven, "Rooting Out Corruption, Building Organizational Integrity in the New York Police Department" (June 14, 1995).

Strategy Number Eight, "Reclaiming the Roads of New York" (November 29, 1995).

Strategy Number Nine, "Bringing Fugitives to Justice" (November 21, 1996).

Strategy Number Ten, "Courtesy, Professionalism, Respect" (August 14, 1997).

1 Jumping the Turnstile

1. N. R. Kleinfield, "For Suspect a Nether Life Spent on Fringes of the City," *New York Times*, 14 June 1996, sec. A, p. 1, and sec. B, p. 4.
2. Mike Claffey, "Ranking Bests Other Big Cities," *New York Daily News*, 1 Dec. 1997, p. 22.
3. Clifford Krauss, "Crime Lab: Mystery of New York, the Suddenly Safer City," *New York Times*, 23 July 1995, sec. 4, p. 1; Clifford Krauss, "Shootings Fall As More Guns Stay at Home," *New York Times*, 30 July 1995, sec. B, p. 1.
4. Brett Thomas, "The Big Apple Bites Back," *Sun Herald*, 13 Aug. 1995, p. 2.
5. David A. Kaplan and Patricia King, "City Slickers," *Newsweek*, 11 Nov. 1996, p. 33.
6. "NYC's Compstat Continues to Win Admirers," *Law Enforcement News*, 31 Oct. 1997, p. 5.
7. Michael Perlstein, "N.O. Police Set to Adopt Big Apple Focus, Tactics," *Times Picayune*, 6 Oct. 1996, p. 1; Kim Bradford, "Police Try Big Apple Approach," *Columbia Flier*, 20 Mar. 1997, p. 1; Joseph Tanfani, "Metro May Steal from N.Y. Anti-Crime Plan," *Miami Herald*, 22 Nov. 1996, p. 16; Hammil R. Harris, "Barry Grills SE Police Commanders," *Washington Post*, 22 Nov. 1996, sec. 1, p. 8.

8. David Bayley, "Measuring Overall Effectiveness," in *Quantifying Quality in Policing*, ed. Larry T. Hoover (Washington, D.C.: Police Executive Research Forum, 1995), 41.

9. Andrew Karmen, "Research into Reasons Why the Murder Rate Has Dropped So Dramatically in New York City," working paper, John Jay College of Criminal Justice, N.Y., 1997, 34–39.

10. Fox Butterfield, "Serious Crime Decreased for Fifth Year in a Row," *New York Times*, 5 Jan. 1997, sec. 1, p. 10.

11. Jonathan Greenberg, "All about Crime," *New York Magazine*, 3 Sept. 1990, p. 24.

12. William J. Bennett, John J. DiIulio, Jr., and John P. Walters, *Body Count: Moral Poverty—and How to Win America's War against Crime and Drugs* (New York: Simon and Schuster, 1996), 14.

13. Neal R. Peirce, "Reinvented Police?—Could It Be?" *Washington Post*, 14 Jan. 1996, p. 22.

14. Citizens Crime Commission, *Reducing Gun Crime in New York City: A Research and Policy Report* (New York, 1996), 43.

15. One area that remains unexplored is the composition of the state prison and city jail populations according to age and risk. It is possible that during the last three years an increasingly higher percentage of the more dangerous individuals became incapacitated, thus contributing to a decline in crime. While this linkage requires examination, one also needs to acknowledge that the police are, perforce, a factor in apprehending and ultimately incapacitating criminals. A study of Pittsburgh youth begun in 1987 reports that 9.4 percent of the twenty-year-olds, the oldest sample of boys (n = 506), had been killed or wounded seriously enough to be hospitalized by age 18–19. Such a youth victim was "more likely than controls to have engaged in serious delinquency, to have been involved in a gang fight, to carry a hidden weapon, to come from a family who owns guns, to own a gun himself, and to take his own gun out of the house other than for the purpose of hunting." Rolf Loeber et al., "Gun Injury and Mortality: The Delinquent Background of Its Juvenile Victims" (paper presented at the annual conference, Criminal Justice Research and Evaluation, *Program Abstracts*, 1997), 17.

16. Pamela K. Lattimore et al., "Work in Progress: A Study of Homicide

in Eight Cities," *Report* (National Institute of Justice), July 1997, pp. 9–10. The eight cities are Atlanta, Detroit, Indianapolis, Miami, New Orleans, Washington, D.C., Richmond, and Tampa.

17. Karmen, "Why the Murder Rate," 139, 141.

18. Lattimore, "Homicide in Eight Cities."

19. Andrew L. Golub, Farrukh Hakeem, and Bruce Johnson, "Monitoring the Decline in the Crack Epidemic with Data from the Drug Use Forecasting Program" (paper presented at the Drug Use Forecasting Site Directors' Meeting, Washington, D.C., June 8, 1996).

20. Richard Curtis, "The Improbable Transformation of Inner-City Neighborhoods: Crime Violence, Drugs and Youth in the 1990s," *Journal of Criminal Law and Criminology*, forthcoming; Alfred Blumstein, "Youth Violence, Guns and Illicit Drug Industry," *Journal of Criminal Law and Criminology* 86 (1995): 10–36.

21. Ibid.

22. Citizens Crime Commission, *Reducing Gun Crime*, 44.

23. Edna Erez, "From the Editor," *Justice Quarterly* 12 (1995): 619.

24. DiIulio quoted in Fox Butterfield, "Crime Fighting's About Face," *New York Times*, 19 Jan. 1997, sec. 4, p. 1.

25. Butterfield, ibid.

26. Peirce, "Reinvented Police?"

27. "A Safer New York City," *Business Week*, 11 Dec. 1995, pp. 81, 84.

28. "Big Apple's Big Assault," *Forbes*, 1 Jan. 1996, p. 26.

29. "Finally We're Winning the War against Crime: Here's Why," *Time*, 15 Jan. 1996, p. 51.

30. Steve Reed, "Number Crunching," *Police Review* 18 (1997): 27.

31. New York City Police Department, "Managing for Results," *Report*, March 1996, p. 1.

32. William J. Bratton, "Great Expectations: How Higher Expectations for Police Departments Can Lead to a Decrease in Crime" (paper presented at the National Institute of Justice Policing Research Institute conference, Washington D.C., Nov. 28, 1995).

33. William J. Bratton, "Management Secrets of a Crime-Fighter Extraordinaire," *Bottom Line*, Aug. 1996, p. 1.

34. Robert M. Fogelson, *Big City Police* (Cambridge: Harvard University Press, 1977), 11.

35. Robert Trojanowicz and Bonnie Buquerox, *Community Policing: A Contemporary Perspective* (Cincinnati: Anderson Publishing, 1990), 3.

36. One scholar observed that community policing "is not a clear-cut concept, for it involves reforming decision-making processes and creating new cultures within police departments, rather than being a specific tactical plan." Wesley G. Skogan, "The Impact of Community Policing on Neighborhood Residents: A Cross Site Analysis," in *The Challenge of Community Policing*, ed. Dennis P. Rosenbaum (Thousand Oaks, Calif.: Sage, 1994), 167.

37. Gary W. Cordner, "Community Policing: Elements and Effects," in *Critical Issues in Policing*, 3rd ed., ed. Roger G. Dunham and Geoffrey P. Alpert (Prospect Heights, Ill.: Waveland Press, 1997); Community Policing Consortium, *Understanding Community Policing* (Washington, D.C.: Bureau of Justice Assistance, U.S. Department of Justice, 1994); Jerome Skolnick and David Bayley, *The New Blue Line: Police Innovations in Six American Cities* (New York: Free Press, 1986).

38. Albert Reiss, "Police Organizations in the Twentieth Century," in *Criminal Justice: A Review of Research*, vol. 15, *Modern Policing*, ed. Michael Tonry and Norval Morris (Chicago: University of Chicago Press, 1992), 54.

39. Mark H. Moore, George W. Kelling, and Mary Ann Wycoff, "Organizational Change and Leadership: Conditions and Strategies for Creating a Culture of Community Policing" (proposal submitted to the National Institute of Justice, July 1995).

40. The organizational variables include specialization, functional and spatial differentiation, centralization, hierarchical differentiation, managerial tenure, personnel diversity, and certain control variables. The external variables include indices of local political culture and community characteristics and community collaborative efforts. Jihong Zhao, *Why Police Organizations Change* (Washington, D.C.: Police Executive Research Forum, 1996), 45.

41. Ibid., 77, 82.

42. Malcolm K. Sparrow, Mark H. Moore, and David M. Kennedy, *Beyond 911: A New Era for Policing* (New York: Basic Books, 1990).

43. One in-depth analysis of attempts to reorient patrol strategies in

accordance with community needs asserted: "The development of patrol strategies has tended to be evolutionary, changing only belatedly in response to new demands from citizens or policy makers. Most patrol systems are self-perpetuating and reactionary in nature, in the name of efficiency they rely on band aid approaches to problem solving in the community and tend to lose track of their goals, substituting means for ends to the point where they are unable to show precisely what it is they are being efficient about—the tail ends up wagging the dog." John Boydstun and Michael E. Sherry, *San Diego Community Profile, Final Report* (Washington, D.C.: Police Foundation, 1975), iii.

44. Larry T. Hoover, "Police Mission: An Era of Debate," in *Police Management: Perspectives and Issues*, ed. Larry T. Hoover (Washington, D.C.: Police Executive Research Forum, 1992); Abraham S. Blumberg and Elaine Neiderhoffer, eds., *The Ambivalent Force* (New York: Holt, Rinehart and Winston, 1985).

45. Egon Bittner, *The Functions of the Police in Modern Society* (Cambridge: Oelgeschlager, Gunn and Hain, 1980), 6.

46. Jerome H. Skolnick, *Justice without Trial* (New York: Wiley, 1966); Arthur Neiderhoffer, *Behind the Shield: The Police in Urban Society* (New York: Doubleday, 1967).

47. Victor Kappeler, Richard D. Sluder, and Geoffrey Alpert, *Forces of Deviance: The Dark Side of Policing* (Prospect Heights, Ill.: Waveland, 1994); Elizabeth Reuss-Ianni, *Two Cultures of Policing* (New Brunswick, N.J.: Transaction Books). A former New York City transit police officer, for example, "was supposed to be society's defender, but he felt less respected than the most humble citizens. He was supposed to represent the law, but he did not feel he could count on the law's full protection. . . ` He felt his life to be a grimy, tour by tour struggle where the respect you got was the respect you imposed and where you could not admit your fears unless you appear weak. This struggle became 'Us versus Them' where Them was both the public and the department. Us was him and his partner." Michael Daly, "Dangerous Lure of Street Justice," *Daily News*, 24 Aug. 1997, p. 3.

48. Dorothy Guyot, "Bending Granite: Attempts to Change the Rank Structure of American Police Departments," *Journal of Police Sci-*

ence and Administration 7 (1979): 253–287. Police organizations respond "to external demands for change incrementally. A degree of innovation is tolerated, while older methods hold on; new items of reform may be adopted, so long as they do not severely modify the ordinary way of doing business. It is always more difficult to eliminate the old than to incorporate the new. As a result, the organizational analyst commonly finds an institution motivated by competing values and in pursuit of conflicting goals." Joseph P. Viteritti, *Police Professionalism in New York City: The Zuccotti Committee in Historical Context* (New York: Center for Research in Crime and Justice, New York University School of Law, 1987), 18.

2   The Pre-1984 NYPD

1. Commission to Investigate Allegations of Police Corruption and the City's Anti-Corruption Procedures, *The Knapp Commission Report of Police Corruption* (New York: George Braziller, 1972), 12.
2. Patrick V. Murphy and Thomas Plate, *Commissioner* (New York: Simon and Schuster, 1977), 173.
3. Eric Pace, "Five Policemen Hurt in Harlem Melee," *New York Times,* 15 Apr. 1972, sec. 2, pp. 1, 16.
4. Robert Daley, *Target Blue* (New York: Delacorte Press, 1973), 534–535, 537.
5. Murphy and Plate, *Commissioner,* 18.
6. George Goodman, "Muslim Minister Assails Police Action," *New York Times,* 16 Apr. 1972, sec. 2, p. 18.
7. Daley, *Target Blue,* 539.
8. James Markham, "Murphy Defends Action at Harlem Mosque and Bars Transfer of White Patrolmen," *New York Times,* 17 Apr. 1972, sec. 2, p. 26.
9. Beyond simply recounting numerous episodes of how the investigation was hampered, this book reflects a viewpoint of police under siege from all directions, including the Black Liberation Army (BLA). The existence and threat of the BLA, which took responsibility for police shootings and deaths, was downplayed by the department. Nevertheless, the dead officers' names were well known to the entire police force: Piagentini and Jones, Curry and Binetti,

Foster and Laurie. The rank-and-file view of a nonresponsive commissioner and a mayor who was seeking the Democratic presidential nomination is bluntly captured in the following officers' conversation: "It all comes down to one thing. This department doesn't care what happens in Harlem as long as there's no goddamn riot. Every other woman in Harlem could be raped and every other man stabbed to death, but downtown all they care about is keeping the lid on Harlem streets. . . . We could make Harlem safer tomorrow. We had horse cops on West 125th Street so shoppers and storekeepers would be protected and what happened? Some black leader gets up on a soapbox and says, 'How come West 125th Street has to have horses and we don't have them anywhere else in Manhattan?'. . . Immediately the department thinks, 'shit, there's going to be a riot.' So they take the horses away. Same thing with the Tactical Police Force. You know what happens when the TPF came into Harlem in full force, they make six hundred arrests a night and some black politician would threaten a riot because so many blacks were being arrested. So the TPF has never come into the biggest crime area of the city. Again who suffers? The people of Harlem, that's who suffers. . . . And things are getting worse. Lindsay doesn't want any riots in Harlem because he wants to be president and the PC is scared shit of Lindsay." Sonny Grosso and John Devaney, *Murder at the Harlem Mosque* (New York: Crown, 1997), 86.

10. Murphy and Plate, *Commissioner*, 173, 175–176, 180–181.

11. Daley, *Target Blue*, 553–554.

12. In this context, Murphy's reaction to the precinct commander's resignation is instructive: "I wondered whether the deputy inspector had been reading the same newspapers as those carrying stories in which I was accused of excusing a racist attack." Murphy and Plate, *Commissioner*, 181.

13. Ibid., 177.

14. New York Police Department, "The History of Policing in New York," *Spring 3100 Magazine*, Nov. 1992, p. 4.

15. "Civil service examinations hardly eliminated the considerable temptations to take bribes or abuse authority. The police precinct structure was symmetrical with the ward system of the local political party and police work provided numerous opportunities for cor-

ruption. . . . Both took profits from gambling, prostitution and illegal liquor sales." Joseph P. Viteritti, *Police Professionalism in New York City: The Zuccotti Committee in Historical Context* (New York: University School of Law, Center for Research in Crime and Justice, 1987), 3–4.

16. Thomas Reppetto, *The Blue Parade* (New York: Free Press, 1976), 65.

17. Ibid., 161.

18. Ibid., 187.

19. To be sure, corruption is an extremely elusive concept, since it is neither a legal term nor present in the criminal codes. The relevant references in the criminal code are to such offenses as bribery, extortion, and theft. Even these references shift in meaning, depending on the jurisdiction and the period of history in question. Frank Anechiarico and James B. Jacobs, *The Pursuit of Absolute Integrity* (Chicago: University of Chicago Press, 1996).

20. Antony Simpson, *The Literature of Police Corruption* (New York: John Jay Press, 1977).

21. Anechiarico and Jacobs, *The Pursuit*, 159.

22. Institute of Public Administration, *The New York Police Survey: A Report to the Mayor's Committee on Management Survey* (New York, 1952), iii–iv.

23. Lawrence Sherman, *Scandal and Reform* (Berkeley: University of California Press, 1978), xxvi.

24. Daley, *Target Blue*, 39.

25. Letter from J. Lee Rankin to Mayor John V. Lindsay (May 14, 1970), Commission to Investigate Allegations of Police Corruption, *Knapp Commission Report*, 265.

26. Daley, *Target Blue*, 41.

27. David Burnham, "Graft Paid to Police Here Said to Run into Millions," *New York Times*, 25 Apr. 1970, sec. 1, p. 18.

28. Ibid.; David Burnham, "City Opens Study of Policing Police," *New York Times*, 24 Apr. 1970, sec. 1, pp. 1, 32.

29. Commission to Investigate Allegations of Police Corruption, *Knapp Commission Report*, 13.

30. Ibid., 4.

31. Murphy and Plate, *Commissioner*, 141–142; italics in original.

32. Ibid., 146.
33. Ibid., 153.
34. Ibid., 110–111.
35. Ibid., 158.
36. Daley, *Target Blue*, 69.
37. Frederick O. Hayes, "Patrick Murphy on Police Corruption," *New York Affairs* 2 (1974): 89.
38. Murphy's autobiography seems to underscore this point in a different way: "During this honeymoon period a new police commissioner can change the types of personnel that become less removable with each passing day. Each day you keep one is another day in which it is assumed that you consider him or her satisfactory." Murphy and Plate, *Commissioner*, 189.
39. Ibid., 157.
40. This presented a troubling situation for commanders who wanted to prevent corruption, but might cover it up if it did occur. Years later, Murphy told a reporter, "We won't assume you are automatically guilty if something happens under your command. But we will thoroughly investigate the methods you used to prevent it, and make judgments as to whether you were careless, or not using your resources effectively." Commanders were not comfortable with this position. "We can't follow every officer eight hours a day when he's working, or the 17 hours when he's off, when he could be into corruption in his own command or another command. That's impossible for us to do." Barbara Gelb, "The Hard Code of the 'Super Chiefs,'" *New York Times Magazine*, 9 Oct. 1983, p. 30.
41. Murphy and Plate, *Commissioner*, 189.
42. For example, while the commission was in accord with Murphy's new policy requiring commanders to assess corruption hazards, it recommended expanding the commanders' vigilance to include evaluations of specific incidents. The commission thought a commander reporting an incident should be mandated to report to superiors and the IAD whether he thinks the "incident is indicative of broader conditions. He should detail the reasons for his conclusion and outline planned corrective measures if needed." Commission to Investigate Allegations of Police Corruption, *Knapp Commission Report*, 237.

43. Ibid., 237–238.

44. They included increased disciplinary options, pension forfeitures, improvements in investigations of recruits, training curricula, legal changes in enforcement responsibilities, and better patrol assignment procedures. Ibid.

45. Joseph B. Treaster, "Neighborhood Cop of the Block Project Is Calming Bedford Stuyvesant's Tension," *New York Times*, 29 Jan. 1975, sec. 2, p. 24.

46. Lotte E. Feinberg, "Analysis of the Planning Function in the Administration of a Municipal Service-Delivery Agency: Case Study, the Office of Programs and Policies in the New York City Police Department" (Ph.D. diss., New York University, 1977), 151–170. The discussion in the following paragraph draws primarily on this in-depth analysis of the NYPD's planning function between 1948 and 1976.

47. Barbara Gelb, *Varnished Brass: The Decade after Serpico* (New York: Putnam, 1983), 270.

48. Ibid., 14.

49. James Lardner, *Crusader* (New York: Random House, 1996), 230.

50. Gelb, *Varnished Brass*, 132.

51. Murphy and Plate, *Commissioner*, 17, 35, 78.

52. Sherman, *Scandal and Reform*, xxix–xxx.

3 The NYPD: 1984–1994

1. The official committee name was the Zuccotti Advisory Committee on Police Management and Personal Reform.

2. David Burnham, "Graft Paid to Police Here Said to Run into Millions," *New York Times*, 25 Apr. 1970, sec. 1, p. 1.

3. Commission to Investigate Allegations of Police Corruption and the City's Anti-Corruption Procedures, *The Knapp Commission Report on Police Corruption* (New York: George Braziller, 1972), 232.

4. Zuccotti Advisory Committee on Police Management and Personal Reform, *Report*, vol. I (New York, 1987), 16–17, 55.

5. Joseph P. Viteritti, *Police Professionalism in New York City: The Zuccotti Committee in Historical Context* (New York: Center for

Research in Crime and Justice, New York University School of Law, 1987), 9.

6. The Mollen Commission's full name was Commission to Investigate Allegations of Police Corruption and the Anti-Corruption Procedures of the Police Department.

7. George James, "Top Officer Says Police Corruption Is Hard to Stop," *New York Times*, 20 June 1992, sec. B, pp. 25–26.

8. It's no wonder that the commission appended a twenty-four-page exhibit, "The Failure to Apprehend Michael Dowd: The Dowd Case Revisited," in which the commission concluded that the "Dowd case demonstrated a willful effort on the part of Internal Affairs commanders to impede an investigation that might have uncovered widespread corruption in the 75th precinct." The "77th precinct scandal of 1986—and the Police Commissioner's response to it— were the seedbed of the failure of the Department's corruption controls. These events sent a clear message that the Department's reputation could not afford to suffer another large-scale corruption scandal." The NYPD's internal investigative unit had received sixteen separate allegations implicating Dowd and his associates during a six-year period. Yet all cases against Dowd were closed "despite the overwhelming evidence that Dowd often acted openly and notoriously and that large numbers of Dowd's fellow officers and supervisors were aware—or at least strongly suspected—that he was corrupt." Commission to Investigate Allegations of Police Corruption and the Anti-Corruption Procedures of the Police Department (Mollen Commission), *Report* (New York, 1994), exhibit 8, pp. 1, 4.

9. Mike McAlary, "The New Serpico," *New York Post*, 15 June 1992, pp. 1, 5.

10. Craig Wolfe, "Tackling Police Corruption over the Years," *New York Times*, 18 June 1992, sec. B, p. 3.

11. George James, "Second Police Inquiry Begins into Drug Dealing Charge," *New York Times*, 16 June 1992, sec. B, p. 27.

12. George James, "New York Expands Scrutiny of Police," *New York Times*, 24 June 1992, sec. B, p. 1.

13. Craig Wolfe, "Brown to Add Inquiry Power in Police Graft," *New York Times*, 1 July 1992, sec. B, p. 1.

14. Robert D. McFadden, "Commissioner Orders an Overhaul in Fight against Police Corruption," *New York Times*, 17 Nov. 1992, sec. A, p. 1, and sec. B, p. 5.

15. Mollen Commission, *Report*, 2–17.

16. Ibid., 5.

17. Todd S. Purdum, "Police Supervisors in Survey Fail to Identify Their Bosses," *New York Times*, 11 Dec. 1986, sec. B, p. 1.

18. Mary Walton, *The Deming Management Methods* (New York: Perigee Books, 1986), 88.

19. Michael E. Buerger, "The Challenge of Reinventing Police and Community," in *Police Innovation and Control of the Police*, ed. David Weisburd and Craig Uchida (New York: Springer-Verlag, 1993), 103–118.

20. Herman Goldstein, *Problem-Oriented Policing* (New York: McGraw-Hill, 1990).

21. Jerome E. McElroy et al., *Community Policing: The CPOP in New York* (Newbury Park, Calif.: Sage, 1993), 8, 175.

22. Ibid., 9.

23. Goldstein, *Problem-Oriented Policing*, 173.

24. These findings of internal resistance and peripheral changes echo studies of national community policing. See Chapter 1.

25. New York City Police Department, *Community Policing Guidebook* (New York, 1992), 1.

26. Lee P. Brown, *Staffing Needs of the New York Police Department* (New York, 1990), 4.

27. Ralph Blumenthal, "Police Plan Puts Safety in Numbers," *New York Times*, 8 Oct. 1990, sec. B, p. 1. Additional police were to be supported by approval in the state legislature of $1.8 billion to fund the city's "Safe Streets, Safe City" program. The revenue sources were a personal income tax surcharge extension beyond 1992, property tax hikes earmarked for public safety, and an instant lottery game that fell short of predictions.

28. Thomas Reppetto, "Put the Cops Back on the Beat," *New York Times*, 22 Sept. 1990, sec. A, p. 23.

29. Lee P. Brown, *Policing New York City in the 1990s* (New York, 1991).

30. Ibid., 21, 23, 11.

31. Andrew H. Malcolm, "New Strategies to Fight Crime Far Beyond Stiffer Terms and More Cells," *New York Times*, 10 Oct. 1990, sec. A, p. 16.

32. Ralph Blumenthal, "Police Plan a New Version of Foot Duty," *New York Times*, 14 Feb. 1991, sec. B, pp. 1, 6.

33. James C. McKinley, Jr., "Anti-Crime Plan Will Curb Violence, Commissioner Says," *New York Times*, 9 Feb. 1991, sec. B, p. 22.

34. New York City Police Department, *Departmental Priorities* (New York, 1991), 15.

35. New York City Police Department, Police Commissioner's Community Policing Assistant Unit, *Reports* (New York, 1992–1993).

36. Ibid., 6 July 1993, 5 Feb. 1993.

37. Ibid., 15 July 1993.

38. George James, "Having to Sell as New an Old Idea: The Cop on the Beat," *New York Times*, 9 Oct. 1991, scc. B, pp. 1, 7.

39. Brenda Rosado, District Manager, Community Board 12, City Council Public Safety Committee, New York, 29 Sept. 1993.

40. Regina Coletta, District Manager, Community Board 7, City Council Public Safety Committee, New York, 27 Sept. 1993.

41. Viola Green, District Manager, Community Board 16, City Council Public Safety Committee, New York, 29 Sept. 1993.

42. Lee P. Brown, *Q and A with the Police Commissioner* (New York, 1992), 1.

43. Lee P. Brown, *Policing New York City in the 1990s* (New York, 1991), 2; italics added.

4   New Faces of 1994

1. Richard Perez-Pena, "Eight Police Officers Hurt in Clash at Harlem Mosque," *New York Times*, 11 Jan. 1994, sec. B, p. 1.

2. Ralph Blumenthal, "Bratton and Muslim Ministers to Meet on Tensions over Clash," *New York Times*, 13 Jan. 1994, sec. B, p. 9.

3. William Bratton with Peter Knobler, *Turnaround* (New York: Random House, 1998), xii.

4. Ralph Blumenthal, "Police and the Mosque: Aftermath of a Hoax," *New York Times*, 16 Jan. 1994, sec. B, p. 25.

5. Ibid.

6. Bratton, *Turnaround*, xiii.

7. Perez-Pena, "Eight Police Officers."

8. Blumenthal, "Bratton and Muslim Ministers."

9. Bratton, *Turnaround*, xiii–xiv.

10. Ralph Blumenthal, "New York Bid to Ease Police-Black Tension Falters," *New York Times*, 14 Jan. 1994, sec. A, p. 1; Steven Lee Meyers, "Giuliani Tries to Move Past Mosque Melee," *New York Times*, 16 Jan. 1994, sec. B, p. 23; Allison Mitchell, "Despite Boos, Mayor Seeks Black Support," *New York Times*, 18 Jan. 1994, sec. B, p. 1.

11. Bratton, *Turnaround*, xii.

12. Patrick V. Murphy and Thomas Plate, *Commissioner* (New York: Simon and Schuster, 1977), 2.

13. Blumenthal, "New York Bid to Ease."

14. Bratton, *Turnaround*, xxv.

15. Mitchell, "Despite Boos."

16. Bratton, *Turnaround*, xxvii.

17. There was a brief reference to the meeting two days after it occurred. Meyers, "Giuliani Tries to Move."

18. Bratton, *Turnaround*, xxvii.

19. Ibid., xv, xxvi.

20. Sonya Hepinstall, "Korean Grocer in Brooklyn Struggles with the American Dream," Reuters, 11 June 1990.

21. "Judge and Dinkins Trade Barbs over Grocery Boycott," *UPI*, Regional News, 10 May 1990 (Internet).

22. Dan Jacobson, "Lawyer Defends Mayoral Report on Korean Grocery Boycott," *UPI*, New York Metro, 12 Sept. 1990 (Internet).

23. In the matter of Boung Jae Jang et al., *Respondents v. Brown et al.*, Appellants Case No. 90–02710, Supreme Court of New York, Appellate Division, Second Department 161 A.D.2d 49; 560 N.Y. S.2d 307; 1990 N.Y. App. Civ 11338, Sept. 5, 1990.

24. Arnold H. Lubasch, "Jury Acquits Korean Cited by Boycotters," *New York Times*, 31 Jan. 1991, sec. B, p. 2.

25. Rudolph Giuliani, "Rumor and Justice in Washington Heights," *New York Times*, 7 Aug. 1992, sec. A, p. 27.

26. Catherine S. Manegold, "Giuliani Takes a Strong Stand on Crown Heights and Arrests," *New York Times*, 8 Sept. 1993, sec. B, p. 17.

27. Richard Pyle, "Crown Heights Ruling Reversed," *Bergen Record*, 23 Mar. 1992, sec. A, p. 4.

28. Kyle Hughes, "Doubt About New York City's Future Colors Mayoral Race," *New York Times*, 28 Oct. 1993, sec. B, p. 21.

29. New York State Division of Criminal Justice Services, *A Report to the Governor on the Disturbances in Crown Heights*, 2 vols. (Albany, N.Y.: 1993).

30. "The Crown Heights Report," *Newsday*, 21 July 1993, p. 24.

31. Robert A. Jordan, "Crown Heights Haunts NYC Race," *Boston Globe*, 3 Oct. 1993, sec. A, p. 5.

32. Manegold, "Giuliani Takes Strong Stand."

33. Todd S. Purdum, "Giuliani Campaign Theme: Dinkins Isn't Up to the Job," *New York Times*, 24 Oct. 1993, sec. B, p. 1; Catherine S. Manegold, "Giuliani, on Stump, Hits Hard on Crime and How to Fight It," *New York Times*, 13 Oct. 1993, sec. A, p. 1, and sec. B, p. 2; Allison Mitchell, "Giuliani Zeroing in on Crime Issue," *New York Times*, 20 Sept. 1993, sec. B, p. 4; Catherine S. Manegold, "Giuliani Finds Well-Wishers in Queens," *New York Times*, 13 June 1993, sec. B, p. 12; James Dao, "Dinkins and Giuliani Split on Public Safety Issue," *New York Times*, 11 Oct. 1993, sec. A, p. 1.

34. Lee P. Brown, *Policing New York City in the 1990s* (New York, 1991), 1.

35. James Q. Wilson and George L. Kelling, "Broken Windows: The Police and Neighborhood Safety," *Atlantic Monthly*, Mar. 1982, pp. 29–38.

36. Fund for the City of New York, *Police Patrol and Street Conditions* (New York, 1981), 7.

37. Michael Hammer and James Champy, *Reengineering the Corporation* (New York: HarperCollins, 1993), 31.

38. William Bratton, "Management Secrets of a Crime-Fighter Extraordinaire," *Bottom Line*, Aug. 1996, p. 1.

39. Bratton, *Turnaround*, 215.

40. Bratton, "Management Secrets."

41. James Lardner, "The CEO Cop," *New Yorker*, 6 Feb. 1995, pp. 45–56.

42. *Economist*, 29 July 1995, p. 50.

43. "A Safer New York City," *Business Week*, 11 Dec. 1995, p. 83.

44. Bratton, *Turnaround*, 215.

45. James L. Heskett, "NYPD New" (case study, Harvard Business School, Apr. 1996), 9.

46. Committee on Implementation, New York City Police Department, *Implementation Report* (New York, 1994), 1.

47. Building Community Partnerships, Discipline, Equipment and Uniform Sub-Committee, Training-Supervisory, Geographic vs. Functional, Integrity, Paperwork for Information, Precinct Organization, Productivity, Rewards/Career Path, Technology, and Training-in-Service.

48. Hammer and Champy, *Reengineering*, 3.

49. New York City Police Department, *Re-Engineering Team, Precinct Organization* (New York, 1994), v.

50. *Economist*, 29 July 1995, p. 50.

51. David Remnick, "The Crime Buster," *New Yorker*, 14 Feb. and 3 Mar. 1997, 96.

52. Murphy, *Commissioner*, p. 110–111.

53. New York City Police Department, *Police Strategy No. 1: Getting Guns off the Streets* (New York, 1994), 7.

54. New York City Police Department, *Police Strategy No. 2: Curbing Youth Violence in the Schools and on the Streets* (New York, 1994), 23.

55. Heskett, "NYPD New," 3.

56. Chris Smith, "The NYPD Guru," *New York Magazine*, 1 Apr. 1996, p. 31.

57. Heskett, "NYPD New," 10.

5   Enter Compstat

1. For example, the seventh book, covering March 21 through March 27, 1994.

2. The fact that this room transfer occurred in January 1995 is significant. This is when Anemone was elevated to Chief of the Department and thus had greater control over department resources. He and Chief Kelleher (executive officer to the Chief of the Department's office) now had the clout to schedule this desirable but underutilized room.

3. The development of Compstat as an organizational unit is itself an important story. In brief, the handful of individuals reporting to the Chief of Patrol and then, in 1995, to the Chief of the Department (when he was promoted), possess vast formal authority and informal influence. They prepare Compstat reports and briefings and receive many field inquiries. It is no accident that Compstat personnel have been involved in the writing of orders and procedures to implement strategies and developments that both preceded and grew out of Compstat meetings. Their wide-ranging responsibilities include developing agendas, selecting practical crime issues to be addressed, suggesting seating arrangements, informing field personnel of forthcoming Compstat issues, and responding to calls for information. The unit serves as an informal information exchange, which both elicits information and alters procedures. For example, at a spring 1996 Compstat meeting, the issue of shootings arose. After the meeting, three of the nonparticipating precinct commanders approached a member of the Compstat unit in his office. They wanted to find out more details so they would be prepared for future meetings. After Compstat meetings identify issues requiring follow-up, the requested reports are delivered to Compstat personnel. Another example of the way Compstat helps the learning process occurred when a unit supervisor asked to be briefed on how the Compstat meetings are conducted, in case he became a precinct CO. When this in fact happened, he entered his precinct command with a running start and did quite well.

4. The acquisition and development of Compstat's hardware and software make an engrossing story. In the first few months of the new administration, Deputy Commissioner Maple had been unsuccessful in getting headquarters to develop "electronic pin-mapping" to track daily crime at the precinct level. He wanted to quiz precinct commanders on their knowledge and crime strategies.

   Maple eventually approached Detective Yalkin Demirkaya, who headed the Command and Control Center. The computer-savvy Demirkaya worked with the computer software program called MapInfo. Demirkaya explained to Maple that it would take about one million dollars for system design, MapInfo software, geocoding, and high-speed modems for each precinct. Each precinct would be able to upload crime data to its boroughs, which would then transmit information to the Compstat office within the chief of patrol's office. Demirkaya developed the system, and the technologically sophisticated Compstat process was born. Demirkaya collaborated with Lieutenant William Gorta and Sergeant John Yohe from the chief of patrol's office, which was responsible for implementing the system. Federal and private funding for 1994 substantially supplemented city funding for computer and software. This included $472,000 in federal crime bill funding and $199,000 in New York City Police Foundation support. In 1996, the Police Foundation provided matching funds for the NYPD's computer mapping project. The project completely transformed precincts' manual crime tracking methods, equipping each precinct with a state-of-the-art computer system to analyze crime trends.

5. Harvard Graphics is used for the arrest graphs.
6. The profiles are now done entirely in the software package called FoxPro.
7. Lee P. Brown, *Safe Street, Safe Cities* (New York, 1991), 3; italics added.
8. "NYC's Compstat Continues to Win Admirers," *Law Enforcement News*, 31 Oct. 1997, p. 55.

6   100 Palmetto Street

1. Wu-Tang Clan, "Can It Be All So Simple," *Enter the Wu-Tang: 36 Chambers*, Loud Records.
2. Ramlho was the lead NYPD lawyer in this case.
3. New York City Police Department, *Plan of Action: Report to the Police Commissioner* (New York, 1994), 60.
4. Ibid., 37.
5. Letter from Robert F. Messner, managing attorney, NYPD Legal Bureau, April 22, 1998.
6. Patrick V. Murphy and Thomas Plate, *Commissioner* (New York: Simon and Schuster, 1977), 218.
7. Robert C. Ellickson, "Controlling Chronic Misconduct in City Spaces," *Yale Law Journal* 105 (1996): 1165–1248.

8. Debra Livingston, "Police Discretion and the Quality of Life in Public Places," *Columbia Law Review* 97 (1997): 551.

9. Nick Ravo, "With Summons, Noise Police Take Boom out of the Bronx," *New York Times*, 19 Sept. 1991, sec. B, p. 19.

10. Rose Marie Arce, "More Cops to Fight Street Crime: But Can They Combat 24 Percent Rise in Rapes," *Newsday*, 22 Jan. 1992, p. 23.

11. At the outset this Northern Manhattan Initiative identified 180 vice drug and paraphernalia locations. Within several months the Raguso and Messner forces forcefully closed forty-six sites and an additional thirty-two after receiving court papers. Ten locations closed on their own. The attorneys were successful in gaining state superior courts' authority to padlock locations with records of three or more uses of drug paraphernalia. This had a significant impact on drug distribution.

12. Nuisance Abatement Law (31 Oct. 1986), section 7–701.

13. NYPD Legal Bureau, Civil Enforcement Unit, *Report* (New York, 1998), 7.

14. New York City Police Department, *The Civil Enforcement Initiative and Community Policing* (New York, 1994), 11. Documents poured out furiously during the first seven months of the new Bratton administration. They were not always entirely consistent regarding the size of the staff. For example, *Police Strategy Number Five: Reclaiming the Public Spaces of New York* (New York, 1994), while lauding civil enforcement strategies, noted a lower staffing level of thirty-four.

15. George James, "Police Project on Street Vice Goes Citywide," *New York Times*, 6 July 1994, sec. B, pp. 1–2; Al Baker, "Bratton Out to Unleash Police," *Daily News*, 6 July 1994, p. 6; *Police Strategy Number Five*, 9, 43–48.

16. Adam Nossiter, "Police Shut Motel in Bronx, Saying It Is Used As a Brothel," *New York Times*, 7 Sept. 1995, sec. B, p. 8.

17. Homicides increased from twenty-six in 1994 to thirty-five in 1995. Shootings increased from 116 in 1994 to 126 in 1995.

18. David Kocieniewski, "No Respite from Murder: City Decline in Killings Is Not Echoed in Bedford-Stuyvesant," *New York Times*, 20 Jan. 1996, sec. B, p. 25.

19. Twenty-five stores were closed through court orders; forty-four were closed during the nuisance abatement proceedings and twelve were closed through owners' evictions of illegal tenants.

20. Jack Newfield, "Sleazeball Vinyl Club Finally Shown the Door," *New York Post*, 31 May 1997, p. 12.

21. As recently as 1993, the NYPD devoted intense energy to patrol visibility. The chief of patrol issued a six-page directive to all commanding officers recommending ways to "increase the number of police officers on patrol and to maximize the visibility of police officers on patrol." Commanders were to focus on high-visibility foot patrol spots (i.e., business districts, subway stations, and transportation hubs) and specific peak population periods, when community beat officers and specialized units would be assigned. The directive mentioned problem solving but omitted any reference to crime reduction. Chief of Patrol, New York City Police Department, *Maximizing Visibility of Police Officers on Patrol* (New York, 1993).

22. This view was, of course, never stated overtly. Yet it was well known by informed insiders and outsiders. One longtime observer of the police, for example, described Brooklyn's crime-infested Bedford-Stuyvesant section in the late 1980s. "Even a casual visiter to the 77 precinct could see there was something inherently wrong at the station house. In a neighborhood where cops were literally stepping over dead bodies and running into robbers on the street, the most that anybody in a position of authority wanted to know was why the number of traffic summonses was down and the precinct's overtime up. The bigger questions went unresolved." Mike McAlary, *Buddy Boys* (New York: Putnam, 1987), 94.

23. New York City Police Department, *Plan of Action: Report to the Police Commissioner* (New York, 1994), 60–61.

24. SATCOM stands for strategic and tactical command.

7   Brooklyn Bound

1. In the spring of 1996, every borough was mandated to conduct their own Compstat meetings twice a month.

2. Dunne served as executive officer in Brooklyn North's 81st Precinct

from the summer of 1989 to the end of 1990, during the tenures of Police Commissioners Richard J. Condon and Lee P. Brown. He was elevated to precinct commanding officer before moving to his next position as commander of Brooklyn North's crime-ridden 75th Precinct. He served in this position from December 1992 until the spring of 1995, spanning the periods of Commissioners Raymond W. Kelly and William J. Bratton.

3. The exact numbers were 10,355 in 1993, 8,979 in 1994, and 8,031 in 1995.

4. Dennis Dugan, "The General Dunne Leads Fight to Reclaim Streets," *Newsday*, 9 Sept. 1996, p. 21.

5. Clifford Krauss, "Police to Start Big Offensive against Drugs," *New York Times*, 4 Apr. 1996, sec. B, p. 1.

6. This message echoed through the reengineering documents, strategies, and numerous press accounts. See Chapter 4.

7. New York City Police Department, Re-engineering Committee, *Geographic vs. Functional* (New York, 1994), 1.

8. Membership included two deputy commissioners, all four bureau chiefs, three patrol borough commanders, four other assistant and deputy chiefs, two inspectors, one deputy inspector, one lieutenant, two sergeants, one police officer, and three private-sector executives.

9. They were Deputy Commissioner John Maple, Chief of Personnel Michael Julian, team leader Assistant Chief Michael A. Markman, Chief of Patrol Louis Anemone, and some borough chiefs.

10. The primary opponents were the chief of detectives, chief of the Organized Crime Control Bureau, chief of the Narcotics Division.

11. NYPD, Re-engineering Committee, *Geographic vs. Functional*, 7.

12. New York City Police Department, *Police Strategy Number Three: Driving Drug Dealers Out of New York* (New York, 1994), 1.

13. Ibid., 8.

14. Ibid., 7.

15. William Bratton with Peter Knobler, *Turnaround* (New York: Random House, 1998), 277. This front-page headline appeared in the *Daily News* on December 11, 1994.

16. In a curious turnaround, Juggernaut picked a lone high-crime precinct for a small-scale antidrug operation to run simultaneously

with the aborted Queens operations. The precinct was Brooklyn North's 75th Precinct, and its commanding officer was Deputy Inspector Joseph Dunne.

17. By the time SATCOM got off the ground, these Manhattan precincts' 20 percent crime drop had already exceeded those of the rest of the city.

18. Although it is listed in the department phone book, Compstat is not an official NYPD unit with an official command code. Nevertheless, Compstat staff members draft reports, prepare briefings, and receive field inquiries prior to meetings. They present or address questions such as the following: What will be major agenda items? What should you be on the lookout for? What are the chief and deputy commissioner focusing on? Sometimes this information is solicited; sometimes Compstat offers it to the precincts. It is a quick way to shift focus and direct attention. (See note 3 in Chapter 5.)

19. Howard Safir, "The Police Commissioner's First P.C.s Post Message," *Spring 3100 Magazine*, May 1996, p. 1.

20. Felony arrests constituted the bulk of narcotics arrests in 1996 compared to a smaller portion in 1995. The figures for April 1, 1995, until July 31, 1995, are 1,322 felony narcotics arrests, 447 misdemeanor narcotics arrests, 2,512 misdemeanor narcotics arrests, 271 violations, 92 felony nonnarcotics arrests, 289 misdemeanor nonnarcotics arrests, and 11 violations.

21. New York City Police Department, *Police Strategy Number Two: Curbing Youth Violence in the Schools and on the Street* (New York, 1994), 20.

22. New computer software, some of which became available through the 1994 federal crime bill, provided precinct commanders and field officers with a systematic approach to data collection and retrieval.

23. The four principles are accurate and timely intelligence, rapid deployment, effective tactics, and relentless follow-up and assessment. They are displayed at all Compstat meetings and reinforced during the discussions whenever appropriate.

24. Under the MARCH program, precinct commanders, civil enforcement attorneys and city and state agencies (i.e., Fire, Sanitation, and

Buildings) jointly bring action against businesses that continually disregard health and safety regulations and endanger the community. The agencies' synchronized summons activities helps combat these community crime hot spots.

25. John Maher, "NYPD Beats the Blues," *Irish Times*, 15 June 1996, p. 1.

26. Some feared that the subway system would also be shortchanged and that subway crime, which had been declining, would increase.

27. Robberies decreased 20 percent, felony assaults declined 8 percent, grand larceny was down 31 percent, and shooting incidents declined 25 percent from the same period of the previous year.

28. Laura Williams, "Crime Is Down in Brownsville: A 73d Pct Projects Plan Gets Results," *Daily News*, 6 Oct. 1996, p. 1.

29. Previously the Public Morals Division and its Social Club Task Force.

30. Dennis Dugan, "Business Is Bad, and That's Good," *Newsday*, 16 Jan. 1997, p. 16.

31. They were Manhattan North, with a 12.23 percent drop, and the Bronx, with an 11.28 percent decline. SATCOM's share of the nuisance abatement pie also dipped in 1997. There was a total of 712 cases in New York City (3 more than in 1996); SATCOM had 144 cases (73 fewer than in 1996).

8 New Skyline

1. Quoted in William A. Geller, "Suppose We Were Really Serious About Police Departments Becoming Learning Organizations?" *National Institute of Justice Journal* (Dec. 1997), p. 2.

2. Barbara Gelb, *Varnished Brass: The Decade after Serpico* (New York: Putnam, 1983), 229.

3. Ibid., 277.

4. Ibid., 56.

5. Ibid., 248.

6. Joe Klein, *New York Magazine*, 2 Oct. 1990, p. 7.

7. Herbert A. Simon, *Administrative Behavior*, 3rd ed. (New York: Free Press, 1967).

8. Ibid., 221.

9. New York City Police Department, *Bringing Fugitives to Justice* (New York, 1996).

10. Charles F. Wellford, "Factors Affecting the Clearance of Homicides: A Multi-City Study" (paper presented at the Annual Conference on Criminal Justice Research and Evaluation, National Institute of Justice, Washington, D.C., July 26–29, 1998).

11. Her Majesty's Inspectorate of Constabulary, "Policing with Intelligence, Criminal Intelligence," *HMIC Thematic Inspection Report on Good Practice, 1997/1998* (London: Her Majesty's Stationery Office, 1997); U.K. Audit Commission, "Tackling Crime Effectively (I and II)" (London: Her Majesty's Stationery Office, 1994, 1996).

12. Jeremy Travis, "Foreword," *Justice Quarterly* 12 (1995): 623.

13. Rosabeth Moss Kanter, *The Change Masters* (New York: Simon and Schuster, 1983), 301.

14. Bill Gorta, "Zero Tolerance—The Real Story or the Hidden Lessons of New York," *Police Research and Management* 2 (1998): 20.

15. Leonard Levitt, "It's a Matter of Priorities," *Newsday,* 17 Feb. 1997, p. 21.

16. Herman Goldstein, *Problem-Oriented Policing* (New York: McGraw-Hill, 1990).

17. Chris Argyris, *Reasoning, Learning and Action* (San Francisco: Jossey-Bass, 1982), 159–183.

18. William Bratton with Peter Knobler, *Turnaround* (New York: Random House, 1998).

19. Craig Horowitz, "What Should Cops Do Now," *New York Magazine,* 20 July 1998, p. 32.

20. New York City Police Department, *Courtesy, Professionalism, Respect* (New York, 1997), 1.

21. George Kelling and Catherine Coles, *Fixing Broken Windows* (New York: Free Press, 1997).

22. Fox Butterfield, "Crime Fighting's About Face," *New York Times,* 19 Jan. 1997, sec. 4, p. 1.

23. John Sullivan, "Taking Back a Drug-Plagued Tenement, Step One," *New York Times,* 16 Aug. 1997, sec. 1, p. 23.

24. Ibid.

25. Fred Kaplan, "A Blockbuster Effort vs. Drugs: NYC Police Barricade Neighborhood," *Boston Globe*, 2 Nov. 1997, sec. A, p. 10.

26. Ibid.

27. Jacob B. Clark, "Taking Back What's Theirs," *Law Enforcement News*, 15 Jan. 1998, p. 8.

28. Ibid.

29. Chrisena Coleman, "Manning Barricades in the War on Drugs," *New York Daily News*, 24 Oct. 1997, suburban sec., p. 1.

30. Clark, "Taking Back."

31. Ibid.

32. James Q. Wilson, "What, If Anything, Can the Federal Government Do About Crime?" in *Perspectives on Crime and Justice: 1996–1997* (Washington, D.C.: National Institute of Justice, 1997).

33. Edna Erez, "From the Editor," *Justice Quarterly* 12 (1995): 619.

34. New York City Police Department, *Chief of Department Training Memo*, vol. 1, no. 3 (New York, 1998), 1.

35. Lawrence W. Sherman, "Evidence-Based Policing," in *Ideas in American Policing* (Washington, D.C.: Police Foundation, 1998), 4.

36. Ibid., 6.

INDEX